MOJO:
THE MOBILE
JOURNALISM
HANDBOOK

WITHDRAWN

MOJO: The Mobile Journalism Handbook

D1556375

MOJO: THE MOBILE JOURNALISM HANDBOOK

How to Make Broadcast Videos with an iPhone or iPad

IVO BURUM

STEPHEN QUINN

Focal Press
Taylor & Francis Group

NEW YORK AND LONDON

First published 2016
by Focal Press
70 Blanchard Road, Suite 402, Burlington, MA 01803

and by Focal Press
2 Park Square, Milton Park, Abingdon, Oxon OX14 4RN

Focal Press is an imprint of the Taylor & Francis Group, an informa business

Library of Congress Cataloging-in-Publication Data
Burum, Ivo.
MOJO: the mobile journalism handbook : how to make broadcast videos with an
iPhone or iPad / Ivo Burum, Stephen Quinn.
pages cm
Includes index.
IS1. Online journalism--Handbooks, manuals, etc. 2. Broadcast journalism--
Handbooks, manuals, etc. 3. Citizen journalism--Handbooks, manuals, etc. 4. Digital
media--Handbooks, manuals, etc. 5. Journalism--Technological innovations. I. Quinn,
Stephen, 1953- II. Title.
PN4784.O62B87 2015
070.4--dc23

                                                        2014044622

ISBN: 978-1-138-82489-8 (hbk)
ISBN: 978-1-138-82490-4 (pbk)
ISBN: 978-1-315-74029-4 (ebk)

Typeset in Akzidenz Grotesk and Franklin Gothic by
Servis Filmsetting Ltd, Stockport Cheshire

If you have purchased an eBook edition of this title, or have no scratch panel on the
inside cover, please email companionaccess@informa.com for your code to gain
access to the companion website.

www.focalpress.com/cw/burum

CONTENTS

CHAPTER 5

COMPOSING VISUAL PROOF ON A SMARTPHONE

—

To make powerful digital videos requires the skill of knowing how to capture and compose powerful images to tell a story quickly – what we call providing visual proof. This chapter shows how to tell a story visually. We recommend camera apps and provide important tips on techniques, and we discuss the pros and cons of shots versus sequences. Importantly, we discuss how to work on location to best cover an event. We also introduce live streaming in HD, via a mobile.

CHAPTER 6

RECORDING LOCATION SOUND USING A SMARTPHONE

—

This chapter describes how to record clean sound using a smartphone while working as a mojo. You'll learn about basic sound recording principles and the differences between microphones. We'll introduce you to the various cables and accessories available for recording sound with an iPhone. We'll also briefly discuss the apps available to help record and transfer quality sound.

CHAPTER 9
EDITING ON A SMARTPHONE

—

Creating multimedia or mojo user-generated stories (UGS) is a multi-planar activity. This chapter covers all the important techniques for doing fast yet quality mobile editing. It includes multi-track, multi-source checkerboard news-like editing from location; working with narration; name supers, audio post-production and rendering the timeline. To cover all the material in a relevant manner we base concepts on the iMovie 2.0 app.

CHAPTER 10
POST-PRODUCTION ON A SMARTPHONE

—

Post-production was the tech-heavy element of video storytelling that could take time and be resource intensive. Once only possible in multi-million dollar online post-production suites, vision and audio post-production can now be done in the field or the back seat of a car using a smartphone, a microphone and a bunch of apps. This chapter introduces the concept of post-producing UGS on a mobile device.

CHAPTER 11
MOJO, SOCIAL NETWORKS AND SOCIAL MEDIA

—

The amount of video uploaded to YouTube soared from eight hours every minute in 2008 to more than 100 hours by early 2015. Yet many of those videos are of poor quality or simply pointless. Mojo offers a chance for citizens and media organizations to create high-quality videos. Social media and social networks are thus natural fits with mojo. You can also use these tools to promote your work.

CHAPTER 12
FILE DELIVERY AND PHONE MANAGEMENT

—

Videos that mojos create tend to be very large files. This chapter covers the routines and practices needed to send these files successfully from the field. It also shows how to maintain your iPhone or iPad so your device does not become clogged with too many large digital files because we cannot shoot video if the device's memory is full.

INTRODUCTION

Ivo Burum

Stephen Quinn

This book introduces a set of multimedia skills and digital tools designed to make citizens, communications students and professional journalists more ready for a convergent change process that's taking place in society. It defines and develops the concept of user-generated stories (UGS), a more complete form of multimedia storytelling created by mobile journalists, henceforth known as "mojos."

Knowledge is freedom. In respect of press freedom we highlight Kovack and Rosenthal's belief that "Civilization has produced one idea more powerful than any other – the notion that people can govern themselves, and it has created a largely unarticulated theory of information to sustain that idea, called journalism" (2007: 193). Hence, this book provides skills that enable multimedia journalists working with mobile phones – mojos – to use digital technologies to:

- **create more confident and digitally literate communities capable of producing local UGS;**
- **connect educational institutions with their communities and the professional sphere via UGS;**
- **create skilled, digitally ready and employable journalists.**

Many news providers including broadcasters like the BBC acknowledge we are about to enter a more socially equitable content-sourcing era. Former BBC Director-General George Entwistle believes this will include more "public service content creation" (Entwistle 2012). Mojo offers a set of digital storytelling skills for participating in this new communications era.

The authors take a neo-journalistic approach to multimedia news, building on the need to base mojo skills around traditional skills. Mojos require what Stephen Quinn calls a multimedia mindset or way of thinking which combines video, audio, text, graphics and stills. And Ivo Burum points out that this multi-planar storytelling approach – where stories can take a little more time to produce – also relies on many traditional journalism skills, including editing on a mobile phone.

One underlying rationale for this book is to provide a road map for training people to create UGS that enhance grassroots journalism by creating an awareness of what Ivo calls a new common digital language. This enables a meaningful link between citizens, education institutions and mainstream media.

This book offers both rationale and praxis for equipping communities, students and journalists with the skills and technologies to enable them to develop their own *transformative* voice in the new media landscape. In doing so it suggests that current shifts in communication technology, practice and pedagogy also create possibilities for a diverse range of groups and media in society.

In his 2006 book *We the Media*, Dan Gillmor says the accessibility of computer and mobile technologies potentially create opportunities for *citizen journalists* to infiltrate mainstream media. However, two years later journalist Charles Feldman in his book *No Time to Think* called the expanding digital content stream a "potential disaster" (Feldman 2008: x). Feldman was alluding to fragmented user-generated content (UGC) resulting from social media and smartphone use and compounded by the always-on, 24-hour media cycle.

While referring to shifts in communications as a modern revolution, Gillmor suggests an important distinction between *communication tools* and *toolkits*. He tells us that technology has given us the "communications toolkit to allow anyone to become a journalist" (Gillmor 2006: xxiii). We contend that this is true only if definitions of technology include a complex set of journalistic skills, without which technologies are not *toolkits*, and merely produces UGC tsunamis of information. In recent times even Internet evangelists like Howard Rheingold and think-tank leaders like Ethan

Zuckerman have recognized this and moved from technologically determinist positions to acknowledge a need for training.

However, author and media analyst Professor Robert McChesney believes the converged anytime–anywhere communication sphere has created a "critical juncture" in our communications history. For him, "revolutionary new communication technology is undermining the existing systems of communications seen by many as discredited and illegitimate" (McChesney 2007: 10). As a result of misrepresentation and hacking, audiences are seeking alternative and more dynamic media sources, which has led to shifts in media revenue, layoffs at established media houses and closure of newspapers around the world.

This has led to frantic trialing of new converged workflows, platforms and business models which include reader-funded soft and hard paywalls, web TV and more outsourced content, to try to make the journalism business more viable. While some analysts view this as a potential disaster others, like McChesney, see it as a short window of opportunity to make the communications industry more inclusive and participatory.

We contend this will only happen if we move from a techno-determinist approach to one more driven by social realism – from being one of the smart mobs to being net smart – an articulated state where the message is to use the medium to its fullest potential. Once past the point of believing that technology is the answer to society's woes, people begin to consider the investment in social capital needed to capitalize on the technology's potential.

But does democracy begin with access or does it also require skills? Is it enough, as Professor Jay Rosen suggests, for the people formerly known as the audience to "pick up a camera"? Or do they also need training to be able to embrace the potential of online communications? Is this the situation the world's journalists are facing?

A low level of employment, a lack of a political voice, and a press that cannot function independently – which drove the people of the Arab Spring to their revolutions – is a common political cocktail in many marginalized communities. Any long-term change to this state relies in part on a more robust educational sphere and, even more, on an independent and free press. It's in the context of this current precarious state that this book investigates the relevance of a skill set and technologies to facilitate a potential community of practice within schools, communities, and the mainstream media. The aim is to create a more equitable and dynamic public sphere.

With the right skill set and access to technologies these spaces have the potential to support a digital communications language and praxis that could, as Professor Manuel Castells suggests, enable such groups to organize the public sphere more than any other actors before them.

In 2013 Ilicco Elia, a mobile pioneer at Reuters, told Ivo Burum that one key to any shared community strategy or advantage, whether social, educational, or business, was mobile. "Social media is nothing without mobile. If you had to wait to get to your computer to talk to people, they wouldn't do it, or if they did, it wouldn't be as intimate a relationship as you now have using mobile" (Elia 2012). But is this enough and does everyone have the same access and skills?

Many citizens are still caught in a *digital divide* – the economic gap in opportunities to access communication technologies. They need access to technology and skills across different geographic and socio-economic levels. The digital divide points to an irony in the current stage of the global information revolution: the contradiction between the promise of the sublime – co-operation and accessibility for all – and the realities of precarity and conflict among stakeholders.

It thus becomes even more critical for citizens to possess the skills to create grassroots user-generated perspectives. This is especially true if citizen journalism is to have an alternative power in a mainstream environment. For this to occur, student journalists will need a new, more relevant curriculum that facilitates civic-minded philosophies and journalism perspectives. Only then will journalism education fill the void experienced by mainstream journalists as they tool up to be relevant in the new digital age. And it's the reason for this book.

STRUCTURE OF THE BOOK

The first three chapters are the most theoretical. They introduce readers to the concept of mobile journalism, develop the role of the citizen in the world of journalism, and describe the influence and importance of forms or genres of journalism storytelling. Chapters 4 to 10 are highly practical and provide an overview of the skills needed to be a mojo: shooting, scripting, recording excellent sound, voice-overs, touch-screen editing and post-production. Chapter 11 links mojo concepts with social networks. Chapter 12 talks about the importance of file management, while Chapter 13 covers the legal and ethical aspects of working as a mojo. The final chapter offers a range of resources for educating yourself further as a mojo.

We hope you enjoy this book.

REFERENCES

Elia, Ilicco. 2012. interview. London.

Entwistle, George. 2012. "George Entwistle: Speech to BBC Staff." BBC. Accessed September 18, 2012. www.bbc.co.uk/mediacentre/speeches/2012/george-entwistle-to-staff.html.

Feldman, Charles. 2008. *No Time to Think: The Menace of Media Speed*. New York: Continumum International Publishing.

Gillmor, Dan. 2006. *We the Media: Grassroots Journalism by the People, for the People*. Sebastopol, CA: O'Reilly Media.

Kovach, Bill, and Tom Rosenstiel. 2007. *The Elements of Journalism: What Newspeople Should Know and the Public Should Expect*. 1st rev. ed. New York: Three Rivers Press.

McChesney, Robert. 2007. *Communication Revolution: Critical Junctures and New Media*. 1st ed. New York: The New York Press.

CHAPTER 1

MOJO AND THE MOBILE JOURNALISM REVOLUTION

Stephen Quinn

SUMMARY

This chapter introduces the concept of mojo, a unique form of video-making created on a mobile phone, and suggests it can empower a wide range of people. Via sophisticated apps, user-generated content can be made into user-generated stories, and these assembled into user-generated programs. The key is training, and the adoption of an appropriate mindset or way of thinking. The chapter explains why mojo is important, provides a short history of this form of newsgathering, and concludes with discussion of why media companies around the world are embracing video (as well as suggesting that mojo is the best form of video they can adopt).

Mobile journalism, which we call mojo, is an innovative form of reporting where people use only a smartphone to create and file stories. These stories are usually videos, but they can also be audio reports or slideshows or photos and text. Stories are filed from the field using WiFi or 4G.

But mojo is more than a new form of newsgathering. It heralds a revolution in the way citizens can operate in the public sphere. With a mobile phone and the skills presented in this book, anyone can create compelling content. Mojo offers ways for people to become more digitally literate and powerful across a wide range of media. Citizens can become empowered to live and work in more digitally literate communities and environments. In a sense these can be seen as new digital communities – virtual or network societies – where user-generated content, or UGC, is created. Teachers can rejuvenate education by showing students how to tell their own stories with only a mobile phone and in the process create civic-minded students. And journalists can find new ways to tell stories and reach their audiences quickly and powerfully.

Mojo stories are delivered as complete packages that Ivo Burum first called user-generated stories, or UGS. The reporter shoots, edits, voices and captions the story from the field. Mojo offers many benefits for the newsroom. Stories can be sent rapidly from the field, ready to be put on the web or on air. A mojo usually works alone, which means a mojo newsroom can have scores of reporters in the field compared with a television crew that requires teams of people and needs bulky and expensive equipment. Ivo has been developing assembled UGS into an aggregate form called user-generated programs (UGP). He describes these as "disparate pieces of UGC that when edited form UGS, which can be curated into powerful television-like forms, called user generated programs or UGP." These formats are delivered via web TV. The mobile or cell phone thus becomes, as Ivo says, the tool for a communications revolution – a "traveling or mobile bridge between platforms."

A mojo is mobile in at least two senses of the word: they work with a mobile phone and they exploit their mobility to file stories from where news is happening. But this magic does not happen without a context and without training. Media critics and futurists once argued that anyone could become a journalist once they had a video camera and Internet access. This is nonsense. It is tantamount to suggesting that anyone can become a Rembrandt or Titian once they discovered a drawing program on their computer, or anyone could become a Hemingway or Dostoyevsky because they have good word-processing software.

Alexis de Tocqueville, the great French historian and political thinker of the eighteenth century, got it right when he said the French Revolution did not come about because the peasants were oppressed. They rose up because they saw what was possible. That is, they became educated to possibility.

Welcome to a potential revolution in the way people can gather and deliver stories (and what journalists call news). Sophisticated apps make it possible to create video news packages entirely on a smartphone but the technology is useless and results in kludge-like content without trained hands holding the device. We advocate for a "neo-journalistic" approach to doing mojo work. That is because the skills of a trained journalist are most appropriate for making high-quality video with a smartphone. We recommend people use smartphones with the Apple operating system, or iOS. That is because the best apps currently available only work with Apple's iPhone, iTouch and iPad. "It's not about preferring one brand to another; it's about application," says Ivo Burum. And this is why, he points out, "most journalists are using the iOS platform which talks to OSX and enables almost seamless cross-platform collaboration." Other useful apps are being created for other operating systems such as Android and Windows Mobile, but for the moment we believe Apple definitely has the edge. Chapters 4, 5 and 6 provide more details about those apps.

People are already making revolutionary or remarkable content with only a mobile phone. Citizens are creating powerful documentaries, promos and advertisements for television and online. Feature movies have been made with only a mobile phone since 2011. Yet we believe we are only at the start of the revolution because people are largely unaware of the potential of mojo work. They need training and skills.

Mobile phones offer a unique and unobtrusive way for citizens and journalists to record video and audio, take stills, identify location via GPS or meta-data co-ordinates, and communicate with sources and media organizations. They can film discreetly in places where camera crews are banned, and use mobile phones to record interviews with people who might be uncomfortable with a full broadcast television crew.

Essentially mobile phones allow citizens and journalists to report the news wherever it happens, without depending on computers or big boxes of expensive camera equipment – in some cases even before the more professionally equipped crews get to the scene.

Figure 1.1 In Aarhus in
Denmark Ivo Burum shot
footage at a murder scene
on his iPhone. Here he is
(left) uploading it, while
the late-arriving television
crew, seen unpacking
their equipment in the
background, were left
wondering how to get the
footage.

Claus Bonnerup

Location-based mobile tools can help people reach more specific audiences. And given the pace of change, we can expect a range of exciting new smartphone apps in the near future.

A variety of types of mojo have been available for some years. The form depends on the mobile phone's software and often reflects the level of training available to citizens. It is relatively easy to stream raw video via free software provided by companies such as Bambuser (bambuser.com). Let us call this "simple" or "basic" mojo. But this video is unedited and can look unprofessional. One of the aims of this book is to offer help to people to make their mojo work more professional and complete.

The most impressive and exclusive form of mojo – let's call it "full" mojo for the sake of finding a definition – is done with sophisticated yet relatively inexpensive apps such as iMovie that allow fast editing via the phone's touchscreen. Indeed, the real magic of mojo comes via the editing, and this is discussed in Chapter 8. With this app it is possible to create high-quality video packages with only an iPhone, iTouch or iPad. "In fast turn around location based editing what's required is an edit app that has two vision tracks, one used for the story cut and one for the B roll," says Ivo Burum. We repeat, we are writing about Apple apps such as iMovie because they are the best-available tools for making great videos with only a smartphone or tablet. As of the time of writing this book iMovie was not available for other operating systems.

When streaming raw video with "basic" mojo the content cannot be edited if streamed over readily available services like Bambuser, it is not exclusive because it remains on the website of the company that provides the software. Anyone who finds the video on the web can copy the source code and publish the video. This is why media houses often build their own or buy proprietary streaming systems.

The revolutionary aspect of "full" mojo is the fact that all work is done on the device – filming, interviewing, editing and creating the voice-over – and then an exclusive piece of content or journalism is transmitted from the field to the studio or newsroom, and then on to the audience. This potentially creates a greater diversity of content at source.

The ability to edit is the key distinction between "basic" mojo and "full" or "real" mojo. With the latter the finished product looks professional and is equivalent to a multimedia package for the web or a piece of television journalism. Content can be sent to the studio or newsroom straight from the field to a supervising producer, ready to be broadcast or put on the web. That content looks and feels professional. That is no accident. It happens because the person using the apps has been trained. A human brain is needed for creativity. Software and apps are merely tools. We cannot repeat this often enough. As Ivo Burum keeps reminding us, "Sending UGS doesn't mean that you don't send UGC; one does not negate the other." We believe that newsrooms can use both, the mojo's raw UGC for breaking news and the unique mojo edited UGS in the later bulletin and behind the paywall.

TYPES OF MULTIMEDIA NEWSGATHERING

We argue in this book that multimedia forms of newsgathering come in a range of types or levels. The first is breaking news. A reporter or citizen in the field shoots raw footage or stills of a news event with their smartphone and transmits it to the news desk or a blog. With journalism organizations, a producer or editor will write a few quick sentences of context, add a headline and put the story on the web within minutes. Or a reporter can stream live video to the web using one of the free or low-priced applications like Bambuser described earlier in this chapter as "basic" mojo, or one of the more expensive proprietary systems.

In the context of breaking news, think of a mobile phone as a Swiss army knife. If you have to fend for yourself in the news jungle, better to have this tool rather than nothing at all. It is a truism of journalism that the best camera you have at a breaking news scene is the one in your hand. A mojo-equipped phone is perfect for breaking news and getting multimedia onto a website from the scene. If the story gets too big for one person, the reporter can always phone for reinforcements.

With breaking news, such as a ferry disaster or an aircraft crash, the story develops or builds over the next hours or days depending on the significance of the story. In Australia this process is described as "story-building." The mobile phone and online are logical tools for initiating breaking news. Over time we add print stories or photo galleries or slideshows or video to the initial story as it evolves. In effect, we build the story from the foundation of the initial piece of breaking news. Increasingly that initial piece is a mojo video report.

Other roles are developing in the world of mojo. The aggregating journalist or producer stays in the office and scours the web for content to associate with a particular story. They link related stories plus interesting videos, photographs and perhaps podcasts to the original story. This is a skill that has evolved as more and more news is broken first on the web.

We must remember that the treatment of any breaking news story depends on that story's news value. News characteristics or news values are much the same around the world. They relate to stories that describe natural or man-made disasters or conflict, involve prominent individuals, have an impact on a large number of people, affect the 'hip pocket nerve' (money stories), represent examples of a new trend or development (usually the first of something), or involve novelty – something odd or bizarre. Many major news stories also relate to something nearby or involve a local community, or significant person in that community. Local is a significant news value.

MOJO FORMS OF NEWSGATHERING

In this section of the chapter we focus on mojo forms of newsgathering or journalism.

In a typical eight-hour shift, one reporter in the field and their producer at the office can produce multiple versions of a single breaking news story: initially a few paragraphs of text for the web, then a slideshow or photo gallery as images arrive from the audience, or are taken by the organization's photo-journalists, and then video as the mojo in the field creates packages with their smartphone. I worked with journalists from the *Sydney Morning Herald* for much of 2007 developing these skills as the print newspaper evolved into a multimedia news organization. Along the way I discovered the absolute importance of developing a multimedia mindset at the same time. People will not embrace new ideas unless they appreciate the benefits of – and/or need for – change. Ivo Burum agrees. He has trained journalists in Australia, Denmark and Norway to make UGS. He found that journalists want to know that they can do it, that their UGC or UGS is going to be used and that doing mojo won't compromise their journalism.

At the same time I learned the importance of providing easy-to-use technology to people. If people perceive tools as being too complicated they will resist using those tools. The ease of use of iPhones and iPads is another reason why we recommend these smartphones for doing mojo work. As of late 2014, the iPhone could already produce high-definition video. In the next couple of years the quality of the images will improve.

In essence, the reporter in the field remains at the scene where news is breaking and developing. They provide different versions of the story for different audiences at different times of the day, depending on the range of outlets they need to serve. Sometimes the news desk will decide the breaking story is worthy of further treatment and will send other reporters to the scene, and commission a graphic artist to create an information graphic to go with the story on the web.

A mojo lets a print-based organization such as a newspaper compete with television in getting video online, particularly as the quality of phone cameras improves. Sometimes the video taken with a mobile phone can be grainy or shaky, and is perceived as low quality. Most audiences will tolerate poor-quality video if the event is sufficiently newsworthy. Backpack or video journalists (VJs) tend to carry better-quality cameras and use tripods to get better-quality video. With the latest iPhones and professional shooting apps like Filmic Pro and editing apps like iMovie, the resulting video is filmed and transmitted in high definition and can look extremely professional. But this usually only happens when the mojo has been trained.

A more sophisticated form of mojo newsgathering can be likened to producing a television feature. In the past a group of journalists would spend several days crafting a piece of quality reportage such as an investigative feature to be screened during prime time. We argue the iPhone and the iPad with appropriate apps and skills enable this form of newsgathering – though some news organizations currently prefer to use more sophisticated equipment such as digital SLRs for this form of reporting. This form of reporting is known as "backpack" journalism or "VJs" and is not mojo. How do we differentiate between them and mojos? VJs carry more expensive cameras and lenses and a lot more gear, as the photograph of a broadcast VJ shows.

Ultimately the executives of news organizations choose the video tools that mojos use. Sadly, sometimes those choices are influenced by budget and legacy issues rather than selecting the best tool for the job. We know of places where journalists are forced to use expensive technology purchased years ago that is no longer relevant or useful because the executives are waiting for the accountants to write off the cost through depreciation. In 2011 I tried to convince one of the biggest media companies in China, the Shanghai Media Group, to consider using mojo technologies. Executives were very impressed with the potential of mojo. But they stayed with their traditional equipment because they had recently spent millions on that equipment and would look foolish if they started advocating for cheaper and simpler mobile-phone technology.

WHY IS MOJO IMPORTANT?

Relative to the cost of television equipment, or even digital SLR cameras, the cost of a mojo kit is low. A perfectly adequate mojo kit costs less than US$1,000. Given that a reasonable backpack or VJ kit costs at least US$5,000 and a television crew's equipment costs a whole lot more, mojo always wins when the cost of equipment is considered.

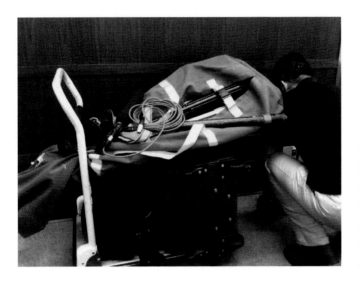

Figure 1.2 A typical trolley of equipment used by traditional television. In this case it's the gear of a TVB crew in Hong Kong. Even without the camera we can see it's a lot to carry.

Stephen Quinn

But mojo has other advantages. It is easy to do, provided the reporter has had appropriate training. Journalists can also film discreetly. Apps are available that appear as if the user is reading a book or using a calculator, which means it's possible to film in forbidden areas and do investigative journalism. Some of the best apps for this include TS Video (TS stands for Top Secret) and Secret Photos KYMS (KYMS is not explained in the app's description in iTunes). Both have lite and paid-for versions so you can try the free lite app to see if you like the app.

Another advantage is the rising number of people who own a smartphone. In the UK smartphone penetration in the general population had risen to 62 percent by the end of 2013, up from 27 percent three years earlier. Indeed, three in five 15-year-olds in the country possess a smartphone. Two in three (65 percent) of smartphone owners access the Internet every day on their phone and 80 percent never leave home without their device. Half of the people in the country aged 12 to 15 have a smartphone. As teenagers become adults they will continue to use their smartphones. This trend is occurring worldwide. The number of smartphones relative to ordinary mobiles is increasing quickly because people in developed nations generally upgrade their mobile phones every 18 to 24 months.

This surge in smartphone ownership has implications for media organizations around the world seeking to interact with audiences. The potential for obtaining good video footage from the audience grows daily as more and more people get a smartphone (though we will repeat until you get bored with reading it that the key is not the technology, but the brain holding that technology).

A BRIEF MOJO HISTORY

It is worth pausing here to look backwards, to see how mojo work has evolved. This might help us understand where mojo is headed. History and experience show that journalists adopt new technologies for newsgathering if the tools are easy to use, if those tools enhance the storytelling process and if they accelerate the gathering of news. The mobile phone is the latest in a long line of technologies that journalists have embraced. The iPhone is a game changer when it comes to newsgathering because it is so easy to use, though the built-in battery is a limitation because mojo work chews up battery life.

The reverse to the above statement also applies: reporters will reject newsgathering technologies if those tools are too complicated to use. Journalists will not waste time with complex technologies. The constant tick of the clock makes editorial staff keenly aware of deadlines. Those deadlines have increased with the arrival of 24/7 newsrooms and online news services.

All of the technologies embraced by journalists since the 1850s, when they first used the telegraph, have reflected the twin desires for speed and increased efficiencies. Indeed, journalism was a leisurely affair until the arrival of the telegraph. Before the technology that *The Economist*'s Tom Standage dubbed the "Victorian Internet" became widely available from about the 1880s, editors published foreign news only after ships arrived. Reporters rowed to newly arrived vessels to secure the latest news, even though it was from newspapers that were months old.

Domestic news travelled only as fast as a horse could gallop, and most news was necessarily local. The pigeons that Baron Reuter introduced in the 1850s accelerated the speed of newsgathering, but pigeons had limited range and scope. The arrival of the telegraph was a watershed for journalism because it was the first technology that accelerated the reporting process on a global scale.

War has always focused journalists' attention on the speed and reliability of technology. The American media historian Richard Schwarzlose maintains that the telegraph turned American journalism "into a news-hungry industry" during the American Civil War of 1861–65: "A craving for the freshest news grew hand-in-hand with the new technologies of steam and electricity," he wrote. Australian historian Kevin Livingston believes the telegraph was the "most significant international communication medium" around the world between the mid-1850s and the 1920s. Indeed, he argued, this period was "the age of the telegraph." In a relatively short time the telegraph's wires encompassed the world, boosted by British capital, labor and enterprise.

On January 3, 1845, a news story made the telegraph famous in England. John Tawell murdered his mistress in the town of Slough, about 24 kilometers west of London. Slough was one of the stations on the Great Western Railway, and the telegraph had been installed alongside the railway lines. Tawell fled by train to the anonymity of London, dressed as a Quaker. But police arrested him at London's Paddington Station. British historian Jeffrey Kieve said that the transmission of Tawell's description by telegraph to Paddington was largely responsible for his rapid arrest. Publicity around the arrest heightened public awareness of the new technology and the telegraph became famous as "the cords that hung John Tawell."

The mobile journalist, or mojo, heralds another watershed moment for journalism. All of the technologies that journalism has embraced since the telegraph have reflected those twin desires for speed and increased efficiencies. The history of journalists' use of newsgathering technologies illustrates this point: tools like long-distance telephony, the satellite phone and portable electronic newsgathering kits used in the Afghanistan and Iraq wars all represent examples of this evolution.

In the years since the telegraph accelerated the newsgathering process, reporters have increasingly sought ways to gather news and get it back to their editors as quickly as possible. That development has been more marked in the recent decade with the spread of converged newsrooms and the 24/7 news cycle. The first mojo experiments in 2007 were a significant development in the evolution of reporting tools. Prior to its merger to become Thomson Reuters, the Reuters news agency was a mojo pioneer from its European headquarters in London, equipping a small band of journalists with a mobile journalism toolkit in 2007. Mark Jones, then editor of Reuters' breaking news service, News Alert, said the company was looking to the future: "We were thinking about new ways to report," he told one of the authors in 2007. Jones said his role was to be more available to the audience, plus he wanted to give journalists technology that was portable and flexible.

Ilicco Elia, at the time head of consumer mobile for Reuters Media, said the mojo project was the start of a new way to tell stories. "Mobile phones allow journalists to swap their heavy camera equipment for a smaller device," he said. A year later Reuters' then chief scientist, Nic Fulton, predicted mobile phones would have high-definition video capability by somewhere around 2011 and

2013. "Five, maybe even three years out, mobile phones could have HD (high definition) video capability and they could have extremely powerful VPUs (processors) and keyboards. I still think that it will ultimately be a very personal mobile device. So clearly, there is potential for it to have quite a transformative effect on journalism," he wrote in 2008. Fulton was prescient.

FINDING YOUR MOJO

The word "mojo" has many meanings around the world. In the world of popular culture, if your mojo is working you have sex appeal. The word hints of power and magic. In the context of reportage, mobile journalism is producing powerful changes to the way online sites report. The mobile phone offers unique newsgathering potential. Online news sites concentrate on breaking news because research shows this form of news builds audiences. Online revenues are based almost entirely on advertising and the "clickstream" (the number of people who visit the site) so breaking news, especially multimedia forms such as video, become vital because they offer the best ways to build audiences, which can be sold to advertisers.

Major newspaper companies are boosting their video content because advertisers want their advertisements associated with video. Advertisers like video because stories associated with it get up to 32 percent more clicks. In 2013 *The New York Times* announced its video operation had become an essential component of the company's growth strategy, along with global expansion and enhanced digital subscription options. "The appetites of advertisers to do video are so great we think our chance to grow our share of the video market is great," chief executive Mark Thompson told investors on a conference call in mid-2013. America's Interactive Advertising Bureau announced that advertising revenues for digital video boomed 24 percent to US$1.3

billion during the first six months of 2013, compared with the same period the previous year.

Rebecca Howard, general manager of video for *The New York Times*, said video streams grew 62 percent in 2013. In early 2014 she noted that it produced an average of 300 videos a month, up from about 250 when she was hired from AOL in February 2013. The newspaper more than doubled the size of its video staff in 2013, from 25 a year earlier, and started producing in-house video in 2005.

Ken Doctor writes the Newsonomics blog (http://newsonomics. com/) about the economics of the newspaper industry and the spread of new media. Writing about *The New York Times* and video he concluded, "the easiest way to grow digital revenue is video." This suggests a strong economic argument for mojo in the world of mainstream media.

The next chapter describes the various subfields of journalism and distinguishes between citizen witness and citizen journalism as well as mojo work. Welcome to the world of the mojo!

CHAPTER 2

CITIZENS AND JOURNALISM

Ivo Burum

SUMMARY

This chapter describes the various subfields of journalism and in particular distinguishes between citizen witness and citizen journalism. It locates mojo within community, education and mainstream media, and identifies how the use of this common digital language is a product of the culture within which it has evolved.

An underlying rationale for this book is to propose a structure for training citizens, students and professional journalists to create digital content using mobile devices. One aim is to enhance the possibility of grassroots journalism via meaningful communication between citizen and mainstream media. This book argues that the holistic storytelling skills taught here could form the basis of a common digital language (CDL) across spheres of communication. Understanding the intersection between these spheres is a first step towards igniting a change process, which enables more diverse communications, in a more purposeful and inclusive *public sphere.* To understand the above possibilities more fully, we need to define journalism, and introduce some of its forms.

Figure 2.1 Citizen journalist from remote Elcho Island in Australia learning mojo.

Ivo Burum

The art of *storytelling* is one of the oldest forms of communication and journalism is one of its more industrial styles. Mobile is an innovative holistic creation and delivery mode. Ask a journalist to define journalism and they will tell you the role of journalism remains what it has always been. In a democracy this is to provide information that's of public benefit, which citizens need to be free and self-governing. Journalism exists as a variety of forms of digital content creation. Here are a few forms of journalism that are relevant to this conversation:

- **Alternative, participatory and citizen forms of journalism are based on citizens playing an active role in the process of collecting, reporting, analysing, and disseminating news and information.**
- **Civic journalism, which can be done by professionals, can be defined as doing journalism to be civic-minded.**
- **Collaborative journalism, which can be done by professionals and citizens together, is often focused around achieving a specific outcome.**

Two forms of content discussed in this book are:

- **User-generated content (UGC) is a raw unedited form that's preferred by news organizations and TV networks because it is easily packaged.**
- **User-generated stories (UGS) are a more developed and edited multimedia form that's discussed throughout this book.**

William Woo, director of the graduate program in Journalism at Stanford University, suggests that: "At its core, the functional definition of journalism is much like the functional definition of a duck. If it looks like journalism, acts like journalism, and produces the work of journalism, then it's journalism, and the people doing it are journalists. Whoever they are" (2005: 1).

Woo's functional definition, like New York University Professor Jay Rosen's belief that "anything that broadens your horizon is journalism" (2011), makes journalism sound like the coyote in a *Roadrunner* cartoon – wearing a different ACME disguise for each job. Perhaps as journalism struggles under the weight of commercial pressure, to fulfill its political role, it has waddled into the jaws of its profession. In the press's ongoing struggle to fulfill its Fourth Estate promise and transcend its commercial imperatives, journalism has, as Australian journalist and academic Julianne Schultz suggests, "taken a battering" (cited in Burum 2014: 27). As a result, Woo believes, journalism may have lost its way: "There is now a widespread and reasonable doubt that the contemporary news media cannot any longer adequately fulfill the historic role the press created for itself several hundred years ago" (2005: 1). This view suggests there is room for citizens to become producers of news-like content and assist with the role that once was the purview of the media.

In the paperback edition of his book, *We the Media*, Dan Gillmor was amazed by "the growth of grassroots media," especially within contemporary news media, such as CNN and the BBC, which "feature the work of citizen journalists" (2006: xiii). Gillmor is right: the accessibility of computer and mobile technologies has altered the scope of journalism and potentially created opportunities for *citizen journalists* to infiltrate mainstream media. In 2006 Gillmor saw this as a grassroots phenomenon growing in strength and power. However, two years later, in his book *No Time to Think*, journalist Charles Feldman called the digital content stream a "tsunami" (2008). Feldman was not referring to Gillmor's early bloggers who were creating an alternative grassroots ecosphere in their expanding *network societies*, or journalists using blogging to connect with their audience. He was talking about fragmented user-generated content (UGC), that results from social media and smartphone use. This has been described by media scholar Henry Jenkins as "kludge" (2008).

While calling these shifts in communications a modern revolution, Gillmor suggests an important distinction between *communication tools* and *toolkits*; a difference we discuss throughout this book. Gillmor believes that technology has given us a "communications toolkit to allow anyone to become a journalist." I contend that this is only true if, when defining toolkit, we include a complex set of journalistic skills, without which technologies are not immediately *toolkits*. Geir Ruud, former online editor of Danish tabloid *Ekstra Bladet*, told me that he saw plenty of university-trained journalists who could press buttons, but who lacked the digital storytelling skills to get the job done: "They know what an iPhone is but I want them to know how to use it to tell exciting stories like they used to with their notepad" (Ruud 2012). In recent times even Internet evangelists like Howard Rheingold have recognized this and moved from their technologically determinist positions to acknowledge a need for digital training.

Marxist philosopher and educationalist Raymond Williams observed half a century ago that we are moving into economies where we'll need a "common education that will give our society its cohesion and prevent it disintegrating into a series of specialist departments" (2000: 34). This observation is especially relevant in the digital age, where mobile devices have the power to fragment and to unify society. With 157 million hours of video content uploaded to YouTube in 2015 (enough to fill more than 18,000 television channels) it's imperative that users are able to access relevant training. Only then will the true potential of the technology be realized.

The relevance of Gillmor's book *We the Media* as a chronicle of the transformation of news in the age of the Internet and particularly mobile is invaluable. Released in a paperback edition just before the launch of the first iPhone, it describes a time where the Internet was seen as an opportunity for progress where "everyone from journalists to the people we cover, our sources, the audience must change their ways" (Gillmor 2006: xxiii). However, at the close of his book, with his optimism tempered by commercial reality, Gillmor laments "the promise was freedom." A freedom that German sociologist and philosopher Jürgen Habermas described as rooted in "networks for wild flows of messages – news, reports, commentaries, talks, scenes and images, and shows and movies with an informative, polemical, educational, or entertaining content . . . originating from various types of actors in civil society, that are selected and shaped by mass-media professionals" (cited in Gillmor 2006: 415).

By 2006 this utopian view of convergence between technologies, platforms and suppliers was being derailed by what Gillmor calls "forces of centralization" orchestrated by government, telecommunications, and even the "pioneers who promised digital liberty" (2006: 415).

According to Feldman the "wild flow" of the convergence of platforms (PC to intimate hand-held mobile communication) and workflows (analogue to multipoint digital) – which resulted in 24-hour always-on content cycles where information travels "faster than the speed of thought" – can only lead to disaster. Conversely, author and media analyst Professor Robert McChesney believes the converged anytime/anywhere communication sphere has created a "critical juncture" in our communications history, where "revolutionary new communication technology is undermining the existing systems of communications seen by many as discredited and illegitimate" (2007: 9). Media scholars Axel Bruns and Pamela Shoemaker believe this distrust of the media, which is partly fuelled by its own gatekeeping practices that determine which news is covered and how, leaves the audience wondering "how can media, facing essentially the same material reality produce different versions of it?" (Shoemaker 2009: 2) As a result of bias, misrepresentation and hacking, audiences seek alternative more dynamic media sources, which in turn lead to shifts in revenue and result in layoffs at established media houses. This resulted in experimentation with new converged workflows, platforms and business models. These include reader-funded soft and hard pay-walls and more outsourced *living* content aimed to make the journalism business more relevant and hence more viable.

Analysts like McChesney view what some call a potential disaster as a short window of opportunity to reposition communications into a more participatory form. This view is now shared by futurist Howard Rheingold who, in his 2012 book *Net Smart*, shifts from his earlier position of technological optimism, where he said it was enough to be part of the switched on *smart mob*, to critical realism: "Right now and for a limited time we who use the Web have an opportunity to wield the architecture of participation to defend our freedom to create and consume digital media according to our own agendas" (Rheingold 2012: 2). His current, more tempered, view suggests digital media will only further our social and political agendas if we learn to exert control over the medium. Like McChesney, Rheingold believes that only when *smart mobs* become *net smart* will they create an articulated state where message uses medium to its fullest potential.

This idea of a social media revolution has been described as a myth that Vincent Mosco calls the "promise of the sublime" (2004: 3), a digital myth that's an entrance to another reality, rather than some organizing principle of change that spells the end of history, geography and politics. In today's more developed digital sphere Mosco, like Rheingold, observes that once past the point of believing that technology will fix society, "people begin to consider the hard work of creating the social institutions to make the best . . . most democratic, use of the technology." What is required, Mosco articulates, is a citizen sphere where the euphoria created by a *technology will fix everything* mantra is followed "by a period of genuine political debate" (2009: 1395). This post by a blogger in New York University professor of journalism Jay Rosen's blog, *Press Think*, describes this state from a citizen's view: "The people formerly known as the audience wish to inform media people of our existence, and of a shift in power that goes with the platform shift you've all heard about. . . . Think of passengers on your ship who got a boat of their own . . . viewers who picked up a camera . . . who with modest effort can connect with each other and gain the means to speak – to the world. . . . The people formerly known as the audience are simply *the public* made realer, less fictional, more able, less predictable" (cited in Rosen 2006). But is it enough to have control of tools if those tools don't include skills?

Equally telling are Rosen's own concerns about the socialization of media: "Were we making something happen, because we decided it was good, or inviting citizens to fashion their own goods? And getting down to the nitty-gritty did public journalism work? How would we know if it did?" (1999: 8). In 1993 when I developed Australia's first self-shot TV series format, *Home Truths*, which gave 20 citizens – formerly members of the audience – an opportunity to tell their own stories on national TV and become producers of UGC, I had the same self-doubts. But one of the participants, Jeff Lowrey, had no such concerns about his experience: "It's my opportunity as a single dad to get my message across that single dads do it just as hard as single mums" (Burum

Figure 2.2 Ivo working as mojo for *Ekstra Bladet* in Denmark covering a murder scene.

Claus Bonnerup

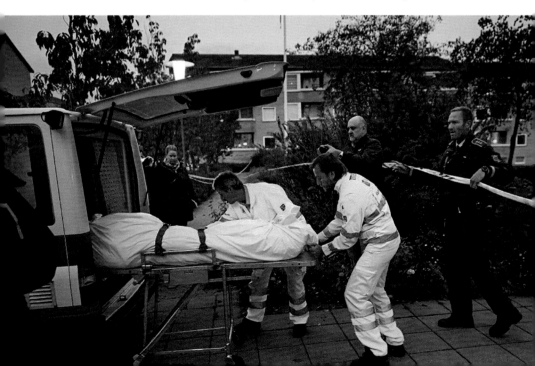

1994). In one sense, Lowrey's short-lived experience and his exuberance is an example of what Mosco describes as the myth of the sublime "that animate[s] individuals and societies by providing paths to transcendence that lift people out of the banality of everyday life" (2004: 3). This is one reason the experience was relevant for Lowrey.

As new breeds of journalism (some of which have been introduced above) plant roots online and define new forms, definitions become a little confusing, especially as we race to keep up with shifting trends and terms. Hence Woo expands his duck analogy by suggesting journalism is an activity that produces product made for an audience and intended for public benefit, "something being important for the public to know in order to make informed decisions" (cited in Hirst 2011: 115). In his book *News 2.0*, journalism academic Martin Hirst asks us to consider the deaths of Michael Jackson or Princess Diana. These were big news days, he says, "beyond the satisfaction of our curiosity" (Hirst 2011: 115). Even without being of public benefit these big public interest stories have a news appeal years later. Hirst's observation suggests we could add one more descriptor to Woo's definition: that a journalist is someone who produces information that is of "benefit for the audience it is intended for" (ibid.). This broadens our definition to enable an investigation of current online content as a form of what Atton and Hamilton refer to as *alternative journalism* that includes *citizen* and *participatory journalism*, which it's argued, is ideally produced for public benefit.

Atton and Hamilton say that alternative journalism can arise out of disenchantment with traditional news coverage and generally represents the views of marginalized groups in society. In another respect, says Stuart Gant, author of *We're All Journalists Now*, alternative journalism is the product of current technological possibilities – in particular the Internet's cheap, accessible, many-to-many interactivity. Its purpose may be to return journalism to "its status as an activity rather than a profession" (Gant 2007: 136) depending, says Hirst, on the environment to which *it* is responding. I would add, depending on whether the activity is wrapped around a skill set. In defining what journalism is, Bowman and Willis provide this observation about alternative (citizen or participatory) content creation: "The audience has taken on the roles of publisher, broadcaster, editor, content creator (writer, photographer, videographer, cartoonist), commentator, documentarian, knowledge manager (librarian), journaler and advertiser (buyer and seller)" (2003: 38). In short, as Rosen's blog contributor suggests, the audience is now the producer and doing alternative or participatory journalism of sorts, presumably geared towards their own, if not always, eudemonic public benefit outcomes. But is the result of this nexus between citizens and multimedia tools always *journalism*?

CITIZENS AND JOURNALISM

Citizen journalism has been used to describe everything from the coverage of the so-called Arab Spring, to the first tweets and images of the Hudson River plane crash, and the crown jewel of American citizen journalism, the Zapruder film. Gillmor is in no doubt Zapruder's film is an act of citizen journalism. However, the film of Kennedy's assassination in 1963 was shot by a man watching a parade, who at best can be described as an *accidental citizen witness*. The film is the result of being *in the right place at the right time* – a raw *citizen eye*witness account. It became newsworthy the moment Kennedy was assassinated and became news when auspiced by media agencies.

Is the above example journalism, or does journalism require an act of constructed journalism – orchestrated filming, editing, a narration that structures raw content into a narrative form for public benefit and publication?

While mobile technology makes us all potential Zapruders, does it make all of us citizen journalists?

Would it have made a difference if Zapruder shot establisher shots and B roll of the scene, conducted vox-pops after the assassination, added narration and structured the raw content either in an edit or a blog, before it becomes – how much augmentation needs to occur?

Does our constant connection to network nodes make the difference?

Is the question we need to ask not what is journalism, but where does the journalistic process begin?

Moreover, is UGC a form of journalism, or does it depend on how it is augmented, by whom and where it is used? Who was the journalist and who did the journalism in the reporting of the Hudson River plane crash? Was it the citizen who recorded the first shots because he was in the right place at the right time? Was that first tweet, by Jim Hanrahan, "I just watched a plane crash into the Hudson river in Manhattan," an act of journalism? Or does news need *some* structure around the information? Did the citizen on the ferry who tweeted what is said to be the first picture of the downed plane need also to tweet more than, "There's a plane in the Hudson" and "I'm on the ferry going to pick up the people. Crazy?" Is here a difference between news and journalism? Was that enough to make it news? Did the journalism occur when the news agency wrapped, integrated and voiced those early smartphone images into bulletins? Or when users on sites like Storify curated the tweets and wrapped pictures, video and commentary around this disparate UGC? Indeed, is journalism the act of augmenting breaking news?

Using Woo's test we can agree that news agencies edited, narrated and published raw pictures in their bulletins, causing the raw footage or stills to take on a news form. But would anything change if the citizen recorded a sequence of shots, such as a wide shot, close-up and cutaways (B roll), or a voice-over (narration) describing what they were seeing, to facilitate an editorial view or process? In my professional view, this could make a difference, especially if the cutaways were shot in a manner to enable them to be used over specific story moments. By choosing specific shots the citizen is editorializing coverage in the same way a photojournalist does when they create a more thought-out, structured, representation of the event. While UGC fulfills a public interest test, the question of public benefit remains unanswered.

The Arab Spring poses a slightly different conundrum. Wael Ghonim argues that deposing the regime in Egypt, where reporters could be jailed for up to five years for criticizing the government,[1] would not have been possible without social media. With government owning interests in newspapers and arresting reporters on the basis of national security social media was the horizontal communications valve citizens used to bypass censored communication structures. This new anatomy of protest, which uses mobile devices to move information quickly, is described as an attempt to reclaim a public sphere through what journalist Paul Mason describes as *Revolution 2.0*. Citizens turned to social media, argues Mason, to create "horizontal links using new technology" (2012: 301). This arguably turned the streets into "parliaments, negotiating tables and battlegrounds" that ignited a collective action citizens had possibly been preparing since the Damascus spring.[2] Google executive Wael Ghonim spotted the picture of a dead man Khaled Said by accident. What he constructed next, his Facebook repository for photos, likes and comments, which ignited what journalist Jose Vargas called a "politically galvanizing Internet" (Vargas 2012: 2), was an act of citizen journalism. Ghonim's posts and links to websites were conscious acts of curation that were published for public benefit.

Were the Arab Springers *accidental witnesses* or *citizen journalists*?

Are their comments and likes on Facebook a form of alternative journalism?

That social media was used to create a first-stage momentum that enabled meetings to design the demise of dictators like Mubarak is probably the revolution's real legacy. But in the weeks following Mohammed Morsi's June 2012 proclamation as Egypt's president, journalists were being arrested and citizens found they were still living under an authoritarian military dictatorship. The revolution might have occurred, but as Eric Goldstein from Human Rights Watch points out, "the laws that Mubarak used to put journalists in prison to control the media are still there . . ." (in Dutton 2012). The report published by the Committee to Protect Journalists in 2013 documents at least 78 assaults against journalists from August 2012 until Morsi's fall on July 3, 2013. If the Arab Spring was the result of a social media revolution, then we can assume the outcome was a few tweets short of the full story.

In light of this, and apart from showcasing a potential for nascent technologies to mobilize and inform, what gains did social media make after the Arab Spring?

Kate Bulkley, writing in the *Guardian* newspaper about the *Rise of Citizen Journalism*, believes factual content creation has become hostage to new "immediate" technologies. She provides an example of filmmaker Roger Graef's use of "citizen footage" to "supplement what he shoots himself." But is Graef's work citizen journalism or is he merely curating citizen witness content to supplement mainstream work? Is Graef's citizen content, as UKTV's general manager of factual Adrian Willis believes, social media being used to provide free hybrid *amplification* around

Figure 2.3 NT Mojos
Gerald Yawulkpuy, Brendan
Yunipingu and mojo trainer
Ivo Burum celebrate their
first prize awards in the
Best Documentary and
Best Indigenous Feature
categories, at the 2011 Fist
Full of Films Festival, in
Darwin, Australia.

Ivo Burum

professional content, in the same way CNN uses raw citizen content from iReport?

While much of the literature on citizen journalism adopts a loose definition, we discuss a narrower, more structured form, called *mobile journalism* or *mojo*. We distinguish between *basic* UGC, which is recorded and published raw content, and the form I am researching, which I call UGS. This is mobile content produced to a broadcast-ready state that is not as easily subsumed by mainstream media's vertical content streams. Clay Shirky writes that becoming media-active is about learning literacies, which "means not just knowing how to read that medium but also knowing how to create in it" (cited in Gillmor 2010: ix). He says only then will we "understand the difference between good and bad uses" (ibid.).

These various forms are discussed in the context of the neo-journalistic approach I advocate in this book. Neo-journalism, which maintains aspects of traditional journalism while embracing new multi-planar forms, is market driven to account for the requirement of developing digital platforms and stylistic choices made to hold audiences. It allows for a multitude of actors with relevant traditional and new skills to be involved in a new, more robust public digital narrative. Conceived in an open space where the recipient takes part in a shared, networked and interactive verbalisation process, neo-journalism suggests citizens can learn the skills to self-editorialize on important public issues, as journalism seeks to redefine itself. My form of neo-journalism is an attempt to create a middle ground, a new dialectic between traditional skills and the possibilities of new technologies that impacts the relationship between alternative and mainstream media, and within alternative media itself.

Today journalism's condition of precariousness, an unpredictability driven by the promise of instantaneous worldwide communication, if still a myth, is one that is difficult to resist. Twenty years after my first experience in self-shot television I am researching the possibility that a more complete set of skills, rather than a *broadcast opportunity*, will give citizens a more sustained voice, and professional journalists more relevant job prospects. Hence my contention that developing UGC to a more holistic, thought-out, mobile digital story-telling form called *mojo* – the production, editing and publication of complete UGS on a smartphone – can provide a countervailing force against a high level of precarity[3] in society.

One way of mitigating the precarity caused by the communication revolution is to understand the relationship between technology and the need for effective training. In 2012, according to mobile pioneer Ilicco Elia, one key to any shared community strategy or advantage, whether social (community sphere), educational (school sphere) or business (media sphere), is digital and, more specifically, mobile. Elia believes social media has a limpid relationship with mobile, which he said provides a revolutionary modern-day "campfire" story-telling experience that "enables you to take people on an anytime anywhere cross platform journey that

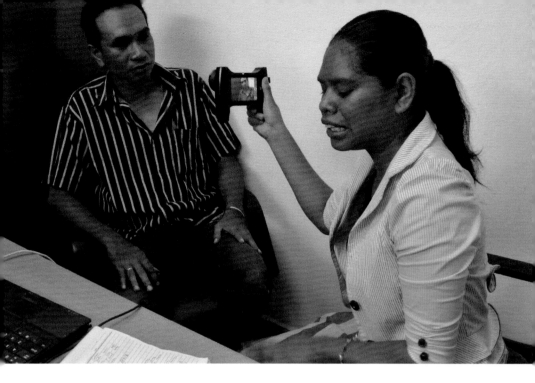

Figure 2.4 **Mojo citizen and journalist Venidora Oliveira reporting for** *The Dili Weekly* **during the Timor-Leste presidential elections.**

Ivo Burum

creates the social in social media" (2012). But is this enough and does everyone have the same access? The simple answer is it's probably not and not everyone is able take the journey.

Even though the Internet is far more social and open to minority voices than print, television, or other broadcast media ever were, access to new digital media training and tools is still marked by inequalities and severe participation gaps. Rosen's blogger may have *arrived*, but many citizens are still caught in a *digital divide* – the economic gap in opportunities to access communication technologies and learn skills that exist at different geographic and socio-economic levels. The irony of the digital divide is in the contradiction between the promise of the sublime – co-operation and accessibility for all – and the realities that suggests that many communities have failed to empower people to employ digital communication technologies. But this is changing. In 2007 just 10 percent of citizens in developing countries were using the Internet compared with almost 60 percent in the developed world. In 2013 this figure is 31 percent compared with 77 percent in the developed world.

McChesney believes the accessibility of technologies and an anytime/anywhere ability to communicate suggests "we are in the midst of a communication and information revolution" (2007: 3). He has no doubt it holds the "promise of allowing us to radically transcend the structural communication limitations for effective self-government and human happiness that have existed through-out human history" (2007: 5). He argues that opportunities are so profound that in future years we "will speak of this time as either a glorious new chapter in our communication history – where we democratized societies and revolutionized economies, or as a measure of something lost, or, for some, an opportunity they never had" (ibid.).

Government legislation and mainstream media may in part deter-mine how this communication revolution impacts citizens and their ability to create a diverse media landscape that includes more local content. But as mainstream media begins moving to occupy new online spaces and its reach and immediacy increases, it's even more critical that citizens possess relevant skills to create grass-roots user-generated perspectives. This is especially true if citizen journalism is to have alternative power in the new mainstream online space.

What's required is a digital literacy that makes diverse online UGS possible. Even with its foundation laid in 1969, the Internet was not effective until it had a common language scaffold, "essentially a set of rules that allows for easier communications between two parties who normally speak different languages" (Pavlik and McIntosh 2014: 212). In 1991 the further development of HTML by Tim Berners-Lee created the web page and transformed the Internet into a global publishing platform (212).

In much the same way, UGS will require a common language and associated skills to realize its potential for enabling digital alternative journalism – schoolyard stories, grassroots commu-nity content, mainstream media news and web TV content – that is balanced and seeks objectivity between events and personal issues. As journalism academic Susan Forde reminds us, this is important because "journalists are human beings, everything they produce is subjective" (2011: 119).

A key to this conundrum is the dialectic that occurs between the audience turned journalist and the professional, and between alternative and mainstream media about the emphasis on telling unbiased stories that are verified. Citizens and students need to learn the skills to tell these types of stories and professional journalists need to be reminded that objectivity comes from being accurate, fair and balanced. It is hoped that the skills in this book will help professional journalists cross the digital divide and develop in students and citizen journalists what Forde calls "a nose for news" (2011: 116). The question is: What is news value and how does this differ across three spheres of supply?

Fraser notes that the idea of an "egalitarian, multicultural society only makes sense if we suppose a plurality of public arenas in which groups with diverse values and rhetorics participate"; a society with a "multiplicity of publics" (1992: 126). Hence, it would follow that there might be multiple definitions of news value between public arenas (spheres) and their publics. Mojo's neo-journalistic approach, which retains the primary skills sets required in any good journalism praxis, provides a common standard. It also enables the personal skills and tools for citizens to speak in their "own voice" and express their "own cultural identity through idiom and style" (1992: 126). It is this commonality that distinguishes publics from enclaves and potentially unites them with "the public at large" (1992: 124), in a more purposeful interaction that maintains their multi-faceted voice.

The purpose of this language is to create a nexus across spheres. Not as one communications public but as three diverse, discursive and transformative subfields of communication where "publics talk across lines of cultural diversity" (Fraser 1992: 126). Like a good

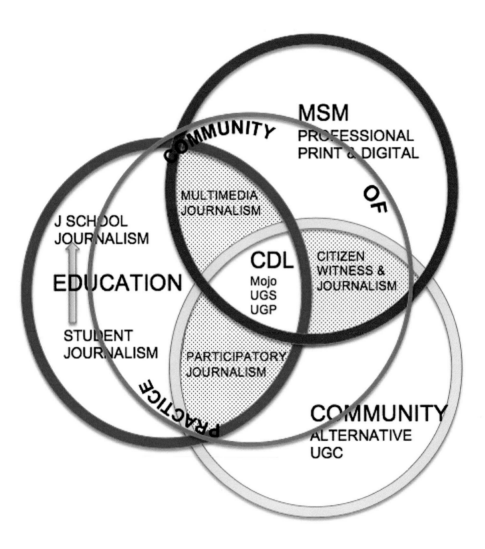

Figure 2.5 **Common digital language and community of practice relationship.**

Ivo Burum

salad, each ingredient retains its individual flavor (outside the dark-green circle in Figure 2.5), but as the mojo uses the common digital language to spoon into the center, they begin to reveal the powerful mix of ingredients working as one. Figure 2.5 describes a hyper-local mechanism for a functioning content sphere. The use of a common language creates a bridge between the spheres, uniting them in a community of practice (COP – dark-green circle), which is generated when like-minded people gather with technology, skills, purpose and a politicized will (Burum 2014).

In conclusion, sustained democracy requires freedom of expression and the protection of an effective public sphere supported by a free press. Without this it can be argued that revolutions only pave the way for another repressive state. Once reporters have soaked up the ambient journalism of revolution and moved on, digital media scholar Associate Professor Alfred Hermida believes one question still needs to be answered. How can new media be used to do more than initiate revolution (which is the "sexy" part that mainstream media usually focuses on)? Indeed, how can it be used to build civil society with long-term heterogeneous visions of a democratic public sphere? In our online world with its networked communications sphere this is an issue that concerns us all. Throughout this book we will discuss the skills and the technologies required to better purpose UGC into more purposeful UGS, produced by professional journalists, students and citizens, to create a more diverse and less marginalized public sphere.

One aspect of this overlapping model described above is its impact on the labor market. Overlapping spheres of labor can initially create exclusion, in particular in new media models, where exclusion can be a result of age, ethnicity and/or geography (Neilson and Rossiter 2005). Job losses can also be the result of new technology that requires shifts in *techne*, which may be a barrier and lead to reluctance to embrace new communications. Addressing this in the news business is paramount and this is discussed in the next chapter.

Define journalism.

The creation of user-generated content is also often referred to as citizen journalism. In this sense, the user or creator of the content, the citizen, generates news-type information and places it on blogs or gives the content to a mainstream media organization. Where does the journalism occur?

What is citizen journalism?

Why do people become involved in citizen journalism?

Can citizen journalism be defined as something that people without professional journalism training do and, if so, should it be?

NOTES

1   Even though freedom of speech is guaranteed in the Egyptian constitution.
2   Members of the 2000 Syrian revolt against declining standards of living and oppression met in private houses (salons) to discuss reform mobilized around a number of demands expressed in the "Manifest 99," a document signed by prominent intellectuals.
3   "Precarity" is used to describe the material and psychological state resulting from high levels of social unpredictability and low levels of labor security.

REFERENCES

Bowman, Shayne, and Chris Willis. 2003. *We Media: How Audiences Are Shaping the Future of News and Information.* Ed, J. D. Lasica. The Media Center, The American Press Institute. www.hypergene.net/wemedia/weblog.php.

Burum, Ivo. 1994. "Birth & Single Parents." In *Home Truths*, edited by Ivo Burum. Australia: ABC TV.

Burum, Ivo. 2014. "How to Mojo: democratising Journalism Skills across Spheres of Communication." PhD exegesis and creative practice, Deakin Journalism, Deakin University.

Dutton, Jane. 2012. "Was the Revolution Lost in Tunisia and Egypt?" Al Jazeera.

Elia, Ilicco. 2012. Interview. London.

Feldman, Charles. 2008. *No Time to Think: The Menace of Media Speed.* New York: Continumum International Publishing.

Forde, Susan. 2011. *Challenging the News: The Journalism of Alternative and Community Media.* Basingstoke: Palgrave Macmillan.

Fraser, Nancy. 1992. "Rethinking the Public Sphere: A Contribution to the Critique of Actually Existing Democracy." In *Habermas and the Public Sphere*, edited by Craig Calhoun. Cambridge, MA: MIT Press.

Gant, Sott. 2007. *We're All Journalists Now.* New York: Free Press.

Gillmor, Dan. 2006. *We the Media: Grassroots Journalism by the People, for the People.* Sebastopol, CA: O'Reilly Media.

Gillmor, Dan. 2010. "Mediactive." San Francisco: Mediactive.com.

Hirst, Martin. 2011. *News 2.0: Can Journalism Survive the Internet?* 1st ed. Sydney: Allen & Unwin.

Jenkins, Henry. 2008. *Convergence Culture: Where Old and New Media Collide.* New York: New York University Press.

Mason, Paul. 2012. "The New Revolutionaries: Experts in Messing Up Heirarchies." In *The Arab Spring: Rebellion, Revolution and a New World Order*, edited by Toby Manhire, 280–283. London: Guardian.

McChesney, Robert. 2007. *Communication Revolution: Critical Junctures and New Media.* 1st ed. New York: The New York Press.

Mosco, Vincent. 2004. *The Digital Sublime.* 1st ed. Cambridge, MA: MIT Press.

Mosco, Vincent. 2009. "Review Article: Approaching digital democracy." *New Media Society* 11 (8): 1394–1400. doi: 10.1177/1461444809344076.

Neilson, Brett, and Ned Rossiter. 2005. "Multitudes, Creative Organisation and the Precarious Condition of New Media Labour." *Fibrecultural Journal* 5: 1.

Pavlik, John, and Shawn McIntosh. 2014. *Convergence Media: A New Introduction to Mass Media.* New York: Oxford University Press.

Rheingold, Howard. 2012. *Net Smart.* Cambridge, MA: MIT.

Rosen, Jay. 1999. *What Are Journalists For?* New Haven, CT: Yale University Press.

Rosen, Jay. 2006. "Title." *PressThink*, June 27, 2006. http://archive.pressthink.org/2006/06/27/ppl_frmr.html.

Rosen, Jay. 2011. "New News." Melbourne Writers conference, Melbourne.

Ruud, Geir. 2012. Interview.

Schultz, Julianne. 1998. *Reviving the Fourth Estate: Democracy, Accountability, and the Media.* Cambridge: University of Cambridge.

Shoemaker, Pamela. 2009. *Gatekeeping Theory.* New York: Routledge.

Vargas, Jose. 2012. "Spring Awakening: Book Review." *New York Times*, Review of Books. February 17, 2012. http://www.

nytimes.com/2012/02/19/books/review/how-an-egyptian-revolution-began-on-facebook.html?_r=1.

Williams, Raymond. 2000. "Culture is Oridinary." In *Schooling the Symbolic Animal: Social and Cultural Dimensions of Education*, edited by Bradley Levinson, 31–35. Lanham, MD: Rowman & Littlefield.

Woo, W. 2005. "Defining a Journalist's Function." *Nineman Reports*, Winter. http://niemanreports.org/articles/defining-a-journalists-function/.

CHAPTER 3

MOJO ACROSS PLATFORMS AND GENRES

Ivo Burum

SUMMARY

Technology analysts are estimating more than 1.4 billion smartphones will ship in 2015 and it's generally accepted that the number of smartphones being used today outnumbers PCs. Mobile is a game changer and for large social and media companies it's a digital cross-screen bridge. Sixty four percent of adult Americans use Facebook and 30 percent of them go there for news. Sixty two percent of Europeans use the social media giant. Globally more than 50 percent of Facebook users access the site via mobile and current studies show that children using smartphones will engage much more with online sites. Mojo content created on smartphones is key to growing and carrying this audience across platforms and screens. This chapter describes one example where mojo is being used to bridge content and transition audiences across breaking news, paywall, web TV platforms and across the home–work–home screen shuffle.

In 1992 when I began developing an early form of mojo, for use on formatted television series, which I called self-shot television, we used DV cameras and large edit suites to create content. Until 2007, when we got apps, mojo was still being defined as raw user-generated content (UGC).

In 2011 when I introduced the Indigenous NT Mojo project at the Global Editors Network conference in Hong Kong, the organizers told me they were happy for me to speak as long as I could relate my mojo to newsroom practice. I lied and said, "Yes I can do that." But it was difficult because the skills I was teaching Indigenous people were still relatively new to a news business still coming to grips with UGC and its shifting revenue stream. The situation is different today as news agencies embrace the holistic nature and the cost efficiencies of mojo praxis and the added cross-platform advantages of UGS.

At the conference Meredith Artley, Managing Editor of CNN Digital, introduced us to "Johnny," their version of citizen journalism – which made me question my definitions of citizen journalism. I also met Geir Ruud, Online Editor in Chief of Danish tabloid *Ekstra Bladet*, who asked me to train their journalists to create UGS. At the conference Ruud approached me and said, "If you can train those people, you can train our print journalists to do that mojo you do and make stories for our online platforms."

Figure 3.1 Indigenous mobile journalists training on Elcho Island for the NT Mojo Australia's first mobile journalism project.

Ivo Burum

"We have seen mobile journalism but not like this," said Poul Madsen, the managing editor of *Ekstra Bladet*, who was with Ruud in Hong Kong. Madsen's background in television enabled him to see the potential of UGS. "It's like creating TV stories that work across multiple news platforms, right?" Madsen wasn't really asking; he knew that mojo was potentially the common digital language (CDL) he'd been looking for to help journalists across the digital divide and to create the cross-platform, cross-screen content that would link his new online platforms.

Madsen and Ruud, like many other print media bosses, were looking to find a fix for their failing print business. They were experimenting

Figure 3.2 Poul Madsen, Managing Editor of *Ekstra Bladet*, with his web TV dreaming vision of the future.

***Courtesy* Ekstra Bladet**

with online news and were about to get into paywall and eventually web TV platforms to try and stave off falling revenues.

Unlike many large media, Madsen and the team at *Ekstra Bladet* had been investing heavily in change for many years because their print revenues were falling dramatically. In early 2014 Madsen told me that "in three years' time we won't earn any money from our newspaper." The comment is a chilling reminder of a paradigm shift that news is experiencing as it moves from print to online delivery. The shift is redefining the news media business.

In early 2012, when I began training journalists to mojo at *Ekstra Bladet*, the emphasis was simply on moving them across the digital divide. Of the 120 journalists I worked with, maybe a dozen had some video experience. And even though 70 percent of *Ekstra Bladet*'s income still came from their paper edition, the writing was on the proverbial wall – go digital or go broke – so we had to make the transition from pen and paper to smart device and screen.

A downward spiral in sales over the past decade led to Madsen's fatalistic attitude to print and his new approach to media platforms and genres. At *Ekstra Bladet* this approach has meant developing strategies across four platforms: print, free online, a paid online section named EKSTRA and a new web TV channel called EBTV. While *Ekstra Bladet*'s print version still makes money, Madsen is betting that – with up to 3.2 million clicks a week, which equates to revenue of 80,000 DK or US$12,500 per week – his plan will work. It's a slow haul but Madsen is convinced it's the way to go: "We have focused on more live television including debates and entertainment and are planning a second studio for live news" (2014).

People are now visiting the *Ekstra Bladet* site looking for a variety of content. When news content is created and re-purposed, across platforms news and the notion of genres or styles of storytelling begins to be redefined: raw disparate UGC works for breaking news, more formed UGS for feature and paywall content and even user-generated program (UGP) formats on web TV. News is developed and repurposed for a variety of audiences and screens.

Mojo offers huge possibilities for enabling journalists and citizens to create content across a range of genres, formats and platforms. However, getting journalists to recognize the need to be digitally healthy, to learn the relevant skills and finally to find the time to work as mojos costs time and money. "It doesn't happen by clicking fingers or a keyboard for that matter; you need to go out and make [digital] stories, try out a few things, make lots of mistakes and then make a few good things from time to time," said Ruud (2013). It also involves shifting generational psyche and the traditional way of doing and teaching journalism.

Massimo Grillo, EBTV's executive producer, told me that change is "an ongoing psychological battle" (2013). Grillo told me that many print journalists are initially reluctant to cross the divide, fearing it will result in shoddy journalism. "It's true we can live with the unfocused shot in a good story – we are web TV," but sign-posting that "your work is not good, but we'll publish it anyway" is a red rag to journalists.

Some senior journalists at *Ekstra Bladet*, AMedia in Norway, Fairfax in Australia and at a number of other media houses where I have run mojo training couldn't see how they would be able to do everything journalists used to do and shoot footage at the same time while still maintaining quality, let alone having time to edit their own UGS. In the first instance this requires a different way of seeing the job; literally a move from pen and paper to a digital notepad, and a *record it rather than write it* approach. This shift requires a mechanism to assuage journalists' fears. In some cases this is a platform to publish more in depth content.

Ekstra Bladet is hoping their paywall site EKSTRA will allay journalists' fears of a drop in quality. The EKSTRA paywall platform wraps traditional and mobile video, audio, photos and graphics around text in a range of new, more complete and at times extended formats and genres. EKSTRA editor Lisbeth Langwadt says it "plays to our quality news traditions, in disclosures, detective journalism, crime investigation, critical consumer journalism, politics and sports" (2013).

A small EKSTRA team works to refine stories from their print stories, focusing on quality journalism that people are willing to pay almost 4 euros a month for (US$4.62). Langwadt says EKSTRA's dual focus is to convert "existing users into paying customers so we can keep creating journalism that matters and, of course, keep our print journalists." Editor-in-chief Madsen echoes this sentiment – "We knew that our jobs depended on going digital" – and he sees this as a primary focus of EKSTRA, to "help keep journalists, produce strong content and make money."

The *Ekstra Bladet* case study is an example of emerging genres that populate new platforms that mojo both enables and needs to accommodate. But the transition from print to digital, journalist to citizen, desk top to mobile platform, across screens and indeed working to keep the audience as it transitions between the home–work cycle has journalists feeling disenfranchised. The experiences of *Ekstra Bladet* journalists are sobering examples of a change practice and how it impacts those caught in its digital crossfire.

Like EKSTRA's paywall subscription model that's being used by many media operators, *Ekstra Bladet*'s new web TV platform EBTV seeks to develop print genres like sport, current affairs, politics, entertainment and travel, just to name a few, into video formats. In the process, journalists' web TV skills will need to develop from story to include long-form program making.

A first step in this journey is to train journalists to become mojos – to use smartphones to create user-generated content (UGC) and then user-generated stories (UGS). Thomas Stokholm, the director of EBTV, told me that one of EBTV's key roles is to help print journalists make the jump from article to program. "TV is a long haul that requires a shift of mindset from the 24-hour cycle to a 365-day operation, where planning is key" (2013). At *Ekstra Bladet* mojos give their news editors and their paywall and web TV producers a number of content and story publishing options. These can be breaking news reports or more developed features that have some shelf life, while others are designed to form segments in longer web TV programs.

One *Ekstra Bladet* journalist, who made this shift across platforms and genres, from print to digital story and formatted program, is Anders Berner, the producer and host of a new motoring series called *Topfart*. "It's a big transition but not as big as I thought," says Berner. "It's actually a nice feeling when you can evolve yourself and your skills" (2013). Berner has moved from creating print stories about cars to producing a weekly motoring program for *EBTV*, which is also segmented into bite-sized UGS. While still on staff to produce motoring UGS, he is also contracted through his own company to produce and deliver the program. "It's more economical this way. I use my own time working around my EB work to make the program." Berner believes this way of working is a growing trend. But like other journalists moving across the digital divide he finds the biggest hurdle is time management: "You can't just ring up a car dealer and get a quote; you need to make time to get the shots and that's the killer."

Jon Pagh, the host of a weekly sports format *Football with Attitude*, agrees, and says enthusiasm is tempered by reality. "If you produce for the paper you talk to two or three sources on the phone and write your story. To produce a video segment you need appointments, you have to inform them [interviewees] before you go, organize the camera, shoot, edit, write the article – basically you are doing everything yourself" (2013).

Figure 3.3 Journalist Jon Pagh in a virtual studio producing *Football with Attitude* for EBTV.

Ivo Burum

It's a big difference that Thomas Stokholm believes requires "someone with a broadcast DNA" to work with the print journalists "who understands the planning, how to work, when to shift to sixth gear." But Pagh adds that making the shift in an under-resourced unit can compromise "the quality of the story, the time you spend researching and the people you interview." Grillo believes that extra staff and training will help, but what's needed is a change of culture. "It's about making TV first and not thinking we need to make the article first and then stick the pictures around it."

Figure 3.4 Ivo training print journalists to cover an interview with smartphones at Amedia in Norway.

Ivo Burum

This paradigm shift from being a 100-year old tabloid to an online platform with a flagship digital web TV presence is both exciting and a bitter pill to swallow. Especially for staff still clinging to old values and workflows rooted in daily news imperatives.

One of the legacies of the traditional analogue way of making the news is a news-heavy front page. All content on *Ekstra Bladet*'s digital front page is still referred to as an article. And because this page can be a yard and a half long (1.4 meters), stories can get lost. An EBTV web program that may have taken a week to produce may be given a spot lower down the site's front page due to its perceived lack of news value. Imagine, says Grillo, if your television program was "pulled five minutes before the newscast and you were told you can run it between 9 and 10pm. Try saying that to a broadcaster."

This clash plays out constantly at editorial meetings where editors choose and shift stories up and down the front page depending on how they are trending. "EB is an old publishing house with news traditions," Berner acknowledges. But he feels "a 15-minute program is a big investment" and needs more time to settle. "If we are only on the front page for two hours we'll only get five per cent of our readers." This is one of the reasons why the paywall and the EBTV platforms were necessary, so that stories can be developed and formatted, to increase shelf life beyond the front page.

Stokholm says people "are coming to *Ekstra Bladet* no matter what," so editors could "think of slowing [the front page] to let the people stay longer rather than read more articles." It's a view – how do we retain the gravitas of the front page while better utilizing the digital potential – that wasn't being heard. Therefore Stokholm persuaded management to let a TV editor with some editorial power work on the front page alongside the front-page news editor. This key new role has the power to tell journalists at the daily story meetings, "You'll need vision on that story because we'll develop that one for TV." Stokholm is seeing an increase in clicks since the TV editor began working with the front-page team.

EBTV plans to create more talk formats, especially a daily live genre studio series like *Huff Post Live*. Produced by the *Huffington Post*, a leader in web TV, *Huff Post Live* features journalists talking over Skype with citizens and experts about the day's issues, a format that resonates with EBTV audiences. The *Wall Street Journal* TV site is another good example of cross-genre cross-platform content. It provides viewers with a number of options including breaking news, more developed stories and a series of formatted programs that are about 15 minutes long. Many of these suffer from being made by former print journalists and are what we call radio with pictures – studio with graphics or stills overlay – but many are dynamic and very televisual.

TIME magazine has taken the platform shift to a new level by creating a production company called Red Border Films. This is a new documentary filmmaking unit and interactive digital platform on Time.com. It wraps extensive *TIME* archives around words, stills and video in a new made for digital documentary genre. While Red Border Films will feature *TIME* journalists and photojournalists, the danger is that at other organizations with lesser resources the digital experience becomes a cheap alternative that redefines video programs as digital chat, which is hosted and posted live.

At CNN the iReport platform uses free citizen content to fill its program holes. Under the umbrella of providing a service to citizen journalism (see Chapter 2), iReport is also a platform for acquiring UGC, often from remote locations, for free use across CNNs program slate. EBTV is discussing a similar concept and platform that invites citizens and students to create UGC and UGS.

Madsen is focused on his company's future and building new platforms. In just two years he hopes to see the eb.dk portal sitting alongside eb24 news and other channels. "We are combining great journalism with our tradition at EB and for me it's a great pleasure to be head of this organization where we can combine doing it on different media, with mobile or mojo at the center of it all. Yes, there's a plan that will give us a great future."

While new platforms can define the style, length and complexity of formats, it's important to recognize that foundation skills still apply. Today it may be cheaper to create channels than it was to produce a half-hour documentary a few years ago. I contend, however, that whatever the genre or platform, the smart operator working in a cross-screen digital content eco sphere will need smart skills that include storytelling, program making and an awareness of social media, which is what we discuss in the next chapter.

CHAPTER 4

TOOLS OF THE MOJO TRADE

Ivo Burum

SUMMARY

A journalist's tools have changed dramatically over the past decade. For starters, the pen and notepad have morphed into a smart device. With a variety of smartphones, tablets and assorted peripherals on the market, knowing what's right for you will require some research. Generally the nature of your project, the time you have to produce the story and how much you are able to spend will influence the mojo tools you choose. In this chapter I discuss the tools that might be in any mobile journalist's tool bag: smartphones, camera apps, microphones, cradles, tripods, power supplies, accessories, live tools and transfer devices. I will also introduce more advanced kit like steady-cams, cranes and drones.

Mojo works on three levels: simple (also referred to as user-generated content or UGC), advanced more complete user-generated stories (UGS) and user-generated programs (UGP). A trained multimedia practitioner, a mojo, using a smart device will be able to produce all these forms. Mojos can be citizens working from their community, students on campus or journalists working in a converged newsroom. Technology has created innovative workflows for producing news-type content and delivering it to the newsroom without the creator ever having to leave location.

I'm often asked: How is mojo different from television journalism? Mojo is journalism in the twenty-first century. Predominantly and initially web based, mojo also lands on television as news, current affairs and magazine programs. Mojo is a more holistic approach to journalism where one operator has the skills to complete the whole job in the field. This is where mojo differs from video jour-nalism. While some video journalists edit on location many return to their hotel to edit on their computer. Then they send their report via WiFi, a broadband connection or via satellite. If they edited on location they might use their smartphone's personal hotspot (if that facility is available) to create a cellular connection with a laptop to send their UGS file. This approach is getting closer to a mojo workflow, which is a location-based, more fluid hand-held response to news than traditional television-type journalism.

Using smartphones enables a journalist, or mojo, to move between evolving actuality much quicker than a larger crew using bulkier equipment. This enables news organizations to cover record-breaking news on a number of fronts, without having to rotate and structure their crews. For example, on *Foreign Correspondent*, an Australian frontline current affairs program, during the Second Gulf War build-up in Jordan riots began east and west of Amman and I had to choose which way to send my crew. Mojo would enable even small outfits to split the crew and record on many different fronts, just like CNN does, but without their resources. Even so, it requires a comprehensive and holistic skill set to enable the mojo to do the jobs of four crew members: camera, sound, producer and journalist.

The other major difference is that the cost of mojo equipment enables almost anyone to have the tools to create UGS. Hence, unlike traditional journalism, which is often paid for by commercially minded oligarchs, mojo stories can be more personal visions of news events told from a community or grassroots perspective.

Journalism professor and media scholar Pablo Boczkowski, in his 2004 book *Digitizing the News: Innovation in Online Newspapers*, notes that most of what becomes unique about a new technology, especially media, usually develops from how users adopt it from the starting point of established practice. How people incorporate revolutionary artifacts like the smartphone in their lives is no different to how people perceived new movies, radio, or recording technology. The pioneers of recorded sound sold their first units as devices for recording and replaying the outcome of a simple domestic activity: someone playing instruments at home. Soon phonographs were used to play music recorded by artists and a recording industry was born. Similarly mobiles have become smart devices that are now being used to create programs and feature films.

Mobile journalism has benefited from this shift. The smart communications industry with its array of apps is expected to turn over almost 30 billion dollars in 2015. Snapping a photo on a smartphone is only the beginning of an evolving online publishing eco sphere. To participate in this online communications revolution we need a thorough understanding of available technology, and even more importantly, a complementary digital storytelling skill set. Limiting the availability of training will restrict the revolutionary possibility of technology. Therefore as communications and specifically mobile technologies become ubiquitous, it will become even more vital that people understand how to use them. But it's equally important to select the right tools for the job.

I HAVE MY SMARTPHONE, NOW WHAT?

In 2015, the journalists' digital tool of choice is the smartphone – a mini hand-held computer that's essentially a pocket-sized mobile creative suite. With almost everybody on the planet packing this much mobile power the question is not so much who is going to cover the news, but who is going to publish first. In part the simple answer is the person who does not double handle – anyone using a mobile smart device with a camera and apps that enable them to edit and publish UGC or UGS from the field.

As far as news is concerned, digital begins with mobile. Knowing what mobile technology is out there is important. Having the right skill-set and an approach that sees current shifts in news as neo-journalistic, rather than some type of new journalism, are important first steps in realizing the potential of new mobile technologies. Strange as it may seem, traditional storytelling skills may be the key to helping print journalists cross the digital divide. In the ever-changing world of digital technology the link with traditional journalistic prac-tice is storytelling. However, being able to detect a useful tool from a silly gizmo is important especially in an app industry worth billions of dollars. With 1,123 fart apps on the market, the following list of must-have tools may help the budding mojo – citizen, student or professional journalist – avoid the smelly ones.

In the new digital newsroom, journalists will be required to par-ticipate in multimedia mojo praxis that involves transforming user-generated content (UGC) into more structured and edited forms called user-generated stories (UGS). While the skills that enable mojos to create UGC and UGS will be discussed in later chapters, the following of mobile tools will help create, augment and publish content. While there are many technologies available, the focus is on the tools and apps that I have used successfully in workshops with print journalists, journalism students and citizen journalists.

THE BASIC MOJO KIT

Mojos can use basic mobile phones that have a camera and get good results. But a smartphone will enable more advanced picture quality and access to powerful camera, editing and journalism apps. If mojos want steadier pictures, with clean audio and the ability to edit on their phone, they might need a version of the following basic mojo kit:

- **recording device (a smartphone or other smart device with connectivity);**
- **mini directional microphone to enable more present sound especially in a live situation;**
- **lapel microphone (radio microphones can also be used in a more advanced kit) because sound is one of the most important aspects of digital storytelling;**

- **rechargeable light to help with image quality in low light;**
- **monopod or light tripod to ensure stability when recording wide shots, doing stand-ups (piece to camera) or long interviews;**
- **mini tripod to help when recording stand-ups (PTCs);**
- **an SD card and an account with a telephone company and/or an Internet service provider (ISP).**

The cost of this type of kit will vary from about US$450 to US$1600 depending on the type of mobile device and microphone. Here is a list of the various components that you might have in a mojo kit.

THE SMARTPHONE

The heart of the basic mojo kit is a smartphone. You can use any smart device that enables connectivity, but smartphones have more accessories and better cameras. The main brands of smartphone

Figure 4.1 **Android and iOS smartphones.**

Ivo Burum

are iPhone, Samsung, Nokia, Blackberry, Google Nexus and a range of others that use the Android operating system.

Your choice of smart device will generally depend on four basic factors:

- **platform and manufacturer;**
- **availability;**
- **cost;**
- **functionality.**

We use an iPhone 5s (or the newer iPhone 6) primarily because there are a number of iOS edit apps that offer two-track video editing, which we believe is crucial when creating news-like stories quickly. If you use a tablet you can use the Video Pad Android edit app and Kinemaster Pro advises it is about to release its Version 3 Android app, also with two-track video editing. While the information in this book relates to most smartphones, here are a number of essential smartphone features needed for advanced mojo work:

- **cellular and WiFi connectivity;**
- **high resolution 8 megapixel camera;**
- **rugged construction;**
- **fast OS processor for remote location upload via 3G or 4G;**
- **relatively small size so that you can eyeball your subject when filming;**
- **access to camera apps that enable greater image control;**
- **access to edit apps that enable professional two-track vision editing;**
- **access to post-production apps that enable control over picture and audio;**
- **a range of sharing and transfer functions;**
- **accessories such as cradles, lights and micro-phones.**

Apps designed for mobile devices generally use an onboard camera (front or back). The back camera of the iPhone 5 and 6 is 8 megapixels compared with 1.2 megapixels for the front camera. Consequently images shot with the back camera are better quality but can use six times more memory.

Ivo's Tip: If MTV taught us anything it's that we are prepared to wear a wobbly shot but not crappy audio so make sure your smart device can accept external audio sources.

CAMERA APPS

Smartphone cameras are electronic and have no movable shutters. The availability of camera apps is often dependent on the platform and the brand of smartphone.

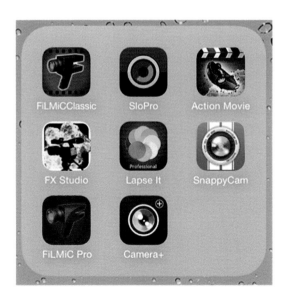

Figure 4.2 Camera apps.

Ivo Burum

We stopped counting iPhone camera apps at 50, but there are more. This chapter will focus on a couple of apps used to record video and still images on a smartphone. Chapter 10 on post-production looks at apps that adjust recorded picture quality.

The iPhone electronics remain constant for every camera app, so functionality is primarily determined by the app and not necessarily the smartphone.

When working with an iPhone make sure that the camera app talks to Camera Roll. This is the media hub where pictures and video live and from where transfers to other apps and online occur. Professional media curation and analysis programs like Xtream use Camera Roll as a transfer node.

Camera apps come in four categories: stills, video, live and propri-etary (apps linked to platforms such as Instagram). We mainly use the native Camera app that ships with iPhone and a number of the apps shown in Figure 4.2 that are used for more specialized work. The basic requirement for shooting video is:

- **an app with manual focus and exposure controls;**
- **a flash and or light;**
- **white balance;**
- **audiometer;**
- **a zoom;**
- **variable frame rates and render resolutions;**
- **a function to enable transfer to various target sites including FTP.**

For a stills camera app you can add:

- **variable image quality settings.**

We will discuss the following camera apps:

- **iPhone camera app;**
- **Filmic Pro Video app;**
- **Camera + stills app.**

Any camera app is only as good as the inputs and or other elements (operator, lighting, audio).

iPhone Camera App

The iPhone camera app records stills and video and is effective for most work. The app has the following features:

- **Panorama, Square, Photo, Video and Slo-Mo Operation;**
- **Burst was an iOS7 introduction that takes ten still photos per second when the white record button is pressed and held;**
- **Zoom while recording video by using a pinch gesture – users are no longer required to set the zoom before pressing the record button;**
- **HDR or high dynamic range attempts to deal with variations of light by taking three photographs at three different exposures which are then superimposed;**
- **Focus and Exposure is set by tapping on the screen to move a yellow square, which selects focus and sets exposure at the area where you tap. Holding your finger on the square locks the focus and exposure. Locking focus is important to stop the camera hunting for focus when shooting at a location where people are walking between your lens and the subject. One of the drawbacks of using the iPhone**

Figure 4.3 Locking exposure and focus on iPhone camera app.

Ivo Burum

Figure 4.4 Filmic Pro screen showing the independent exposure ring and focus square.

Ivo Burum

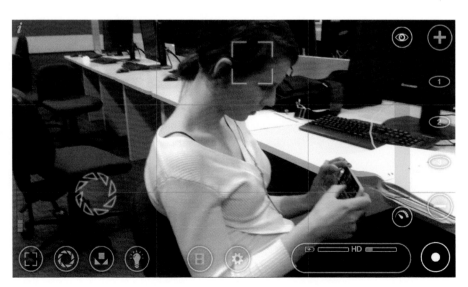

camera app is its inability to set and lock focus and exposure independently of each other. For this you need a more advanced app.

Filmic Pro

Filmic Pro is one of the most advanced video camera apps on the market and is used for more sophisticated work.

The key features that make this app a stand-out video recording app are:

- *Independent control over focus, exposure and white balance.* **This feature is especially helpful when filming a dark unmovable subject against a light background (window). The user can zoom or track in close on the subject, set and lock exposure, track back out to frame the wider interview shot, then locking focus.**
- *Real time 4x zoom with a speed toggle and three key frame settings.* **Zoom is digital and degrades the shot but the key frame enables frames to be chosen for studio-type interview set-ups.**
- *Image stabilization* **is helpful to reduce shake when recording hand held but it does cause the camera to slow down.**
- *Thirds guide* **is very helpful when balancing a frame with people and other elements.**
- *Audiometer* **indicates that audio is being recorded and at what level. This is an especially important check for when the user is not wearing headphones and using external microphones that require batteries. If the audiometer stops working, you can tell that something is wrong**

- *Variable frame rates* **with presets and selector wheel are important when shooting in PAL or NTSC regions and assists when a video consists of archive that has been shot at a particular rate;**
- **Variable video compression bit rate from 12 mbit/ sec to 50 mbit/sec (broadcast is 24 to 50 mbit/sec).**
- **Variable video render resolution up to 1920 x 1080.**
- **Saves media to Camera Roll.**
- **Variable target sights including social media and FTP.**

Filmic Pro has many other features that enable even more advanced approaches to recording video on a smartphone.

Camera +

This app is probably the best still camera app on the market and is available for both iOS and Android systems. Its features enable high-level creative control of the image before and after exposure.

Key features of this app are:

- *Settings:* **provides access to a variety of functions including zoom, geo tagging, grid, the horizon level and picture quality. The settings menu has many other functions and you will need to experiment to determine which are useful.**
- *Gear:* **tapping this menu reveals some very useful options such as Framing, Timer, Burst and Stabilizer – it only snaps a picture when you are holding the device steady.**
- *Exposure compensation:* **in increments from -2EV to +2EV**
- *WB:* **enables you to set the white balance when moving between indoor and outdoor shooting**

- *Lightbox:* is an excellent tool for photographers who want professional creative control over Brightness, Saturation, Grain, Tint, Focus, Rotate, Flip, Straighten, Sharpen, Vignette and a few other controls
- *Focus and Exposure:* are activated by a two-finger tap. When locked the icons disappear from the screen leaving more real estate for you to frame the shot.

SOUND APPS

There are a large number to choose from. We have selected a few that will help you record clean audio on the iPhone, if used correctly.

Figure 4.5 A variety of sound apps that we have used.

Ivo Burum

75

Rode Rec

Rode Rec is a favorite. It's easy to use with many equalization (EQ) and enhancement features that include:

- **compression and expansion;**
- **gain;**
- **hi and low pass filters;**
- **various send features including FTP.**

Voice Memos

Voice Memos provides an effective edit feature that enables the user to cut the recorded track, but there are no controls over audio quality.

Quick Voice

Quick Voice doesn't have edit functions but does enable choice of audio quality. Both this and Voice Memo include a facility for transferring the recorded media to email and social media.

n-Track Studio

N-Track Studio is an advanced multi-track recording app with a number of in-app purchase options that include an excellent Midi module. What we like is:

- **finger pinch and size audio track to enable fine selection;**
- **stereo: switch between mono, stereo x 2 mono and stereo;**
- **frequency: record variable frequency up to 192000;**

- **input setting: select mics, pattern and gain;**
- **multi-track: enables greater control over post-produced audio in particular music tracks.**

Voca Live

If you like to record singing, Voca Live is the professional practicing, performing and recording vocal processor for the iPhone, iPod touch and iPad. With this app you can record (single or multi-track) audio. It features a studio section that lets you record and edit audio with the advanced flexibility and precision of a DAW-style interface (see Chapter 10 for an explanation of multi-track audio).

Location audio is generally recorded with video except when recording narration. But because all audio is recorded digitally narration can be recorded as video and audio. Once recorded the audio is detached from the video and used as narration.

MICROPHONES

Sound is crucial to any video story. In television the quality of sound can determine whether a program is broadcast or not. In the online publishing world sound should be treated with as much importance as video, especially now that online content is being used in web TV formats. While Chapter 6 discusses microphone technique, below is a list of microphone options and suggested applications.

Directional or super cardioid microphones

Directional or super cardioid microphones help record relevant sound that occurs in front of the microphone and exclude peripheral noise. These microphones can cost anywhere from US$25 to US$2500.

- *Rode Video Pro:* **At AU$240 this mic is in the upper limits of what you'd have to pay but provides excellent sound recording with selectable attenuation.**
- *Sennheiser MKE400.* **At AU$200 it is slightly cheaper, has a steel body and is slightly smaller than the Rode.**
- *mCamLite Mic.* **This US$30 microphone that ships with the mCAMLite is a good fail-safe or backup device.**

Ivo's Tip: When recording in a location that includes loud music use a shotgun mic with attenuation.

Lapel Microphones

Lapel microphones, which are called lavalieres, clip onto an interviewee's lapel and can cost between US$40 and US$700. Some of the best are:

- *SmartLav +* **by Rode. A terrific lavaliere microphone for AU$65 but make sure you buy the "+". You may need to purchase a one- to two-meter extension for any lapel microphone.**
- *MXL FR355* **is a lapel kit that includes two microphones – one with a cardoid, or more directional pattern, the other an omni. The MXL microphones require a 48v phantom power source.**

Radio Microphones

Radio microphones can cost upwards of US$300 and you will need to make sure that the mics you choose work with your type of smart device. While most smartphones use a TRS (two-ring) plug, Apple devices use TRRS (three-ring plug) and you may need an adaptor or splitter cables to make the microphone you choose work with your smart device.

We discuss all of the above microphones and how to use them best to record clean sound in more detail in Chapter 6 and in Chapter 10 on post-production.

MIXERS

We have tested the Roland Duo Capture EX, a two-channel USB interface that is compatible with iPhone and iPad. When used with the right recording app (see Chapter 10) two audio tracks can be recorded and monitored, which are outputted as one file.

Figure 4.6 Using an interface device will enable multi-track recording as long as you record on multi-track device.

CRADLES

A cradle is a device that helps steady the iPhone. Here we look at five examples.

mCamLite   Rode Grip

Smart Phocus

Manfrotto Klyp

Figure 4.7 There are a number of smartphone stabilizing cradles; some are device specific and others like the very simple Shoulderpod S1 are adjustable and can be used across the smartphone range.

Action Life Media, Rode, Manfrotto, Smartphocus

Figure 4.8 Shoulderpod S1 adjustable smartphone cradle.

Courtesy Shoulderpod

mCAMLite

MCAMLite is a sturdy aluminum cradle for the smartphone. It provides stability and attachment points for a light, microphone and tripod or monopod. The device, also available for iPods, is produced by ALM. Its weight provides the stability needed to create smooth pans and tilts while handholding the smartphone. You can buy an adapter to attach Canon or Nikon SLR lenses. The price is US$129. The advantage of the mCam brand is their large list of attachments that turn the smartphone into a mini-grips truck. It's smartphone specific and only available for a number of phones.

Smart Phocus

Figure 4.9 The mCam list of attachments includes dollies, magic arms, lenses and lens adaptors.

Courtesy of Action Life Media

Smart Phocus, the cheaper plastic version of the mCAMLite, can be ordered with up to five lenses. A comparable two-lens bundle costs US$109. Unlike the mCAMLite the Smart Phocus does not use a silicone case to secure the iPhone. So be careful that the smartphone doesn't slip out of the cradle. But this is a great system for the price.

Rode Grip

Rode Grip is a smaller cradle, which we love. Not much larger than a cigarette lighter, it comes with three lenses neatly hidden in the case that also transforms into a handle and a stand. We would have preferred it in metal. At US$80 it is terrific value with plenty of wiggle room for a price hike and a metal version.

Manfrotto Klyp

Manfrotto Klyp is a hard plastic housing that clips onto the iPhone and has an attachment feature for a tripod and light. The Klyp supports a range of lights. Price is US$75.

Joby Grip Tight Micro

Joby Grip Tight Micro is a favorite because it embraces a variety of smartphones and compact cameras simply by expanding the grip and snapping it around the device. It's very quick and, at US$17, very cheap. Perfect for using on a second device to hold your autocue.

Shoulderpod S1

Shoulderpod S1 expands and contracts to take any size smartphone. It has a nice weighty handle and I think it is becoming my most used cradle. I love that it is cheap at US$35 and is so versatile. It is perfectly priced for students.

Ivo's Tip: Even if you don't attach gear to the mCAMLite its weight helps keep the smartphone steady when panning and tilting.

Table 4.1 Cradles and a list of features

Device	Features	Lenses	Mount Points
mCAMLite	Weight and metal finish	Yes	Yes Multiple
Smart Phocus	Plastic, device can slip out	Yes	Yes Multiple
Rode Grip	Packs tiny, is a stand, lenses in pack	Yes	Yes One
Manfrotto Klyp	Remains on device, articulated pocket stand accessory	Yes	No
Joby Grip Tight Micro Stand	Fast actuating, multi-platform	No	No
Shoulderpod S1	Fixes on a tripod, filmmakers grip and works as a stand	No	Yes

EDIT APPS

Mojo editing is done on a mobile device using powerful edit apps. Much of the noise about which edit app is best happens because of a technological determinist approach to mobile journalism and *digital trainer skill lag*. Some trainers prefer to use simple apps because, like many print journalists we work with, they have not been trained to create multi-planar, multi-media UGS. Mobile journalism – like all journalism – is based on storytelling and not technology. The easiest way to assemble story vision on a non-linear timeline is to use two tracks of video – one track for the story, the other for B roll. So in this section we concentrate on edit apps that have two vision tracks.

Figure 4.10 **iMovie 2.0, Voddio, Cute Cut Pro and VideoPad.**

Ivo Burum

iMovie 2.0   Voddio   Cute Cut Pro   VideoPad

The most professional edit apps for iOS devices are iMovie 2.0 from Apple and Voddio from VeriCorder. Both offer two video tracks, which is essential for editing stories quickly (see Chapter 9). Cute Cut Pro offers two video tracks on iOS devices and a seemingly infinite number of picture (stills) tracks (we stopped counting at ten) making it ideal for creating composite sub-clip packages. As this book was being produced the VideoPad editor, which is only available for tablets, is the only iOS, Android and Windows app with multi-track video editing. The maker of KineMaster has advised that by the time this book is printed they will have released a two-vision track edit app for Android smart-phones called KineMaster Pro.

The above apps offer features that include video and audio import, and enable finished stories to be rendered and exported at multiple resolutions. The apps enable content upload to social media sites via WiFi or 3G/4G.

Table 4.2 lists the apps we tested.

We use iMovie 2.0 almost exclusively because many participants in our training courses are familiar with iOS. We suggest that you try the above apps and decide which works best for you. If you need the added features from one app you can make sub clips and import back and forth between apps.

In particular we like two Voddio features: the first enables all tracks to slide left and right along the timeline and is arguably one of the most important features in professional non-linear editing because it enables completed stories to be adjusted at any point along the timeline without unstitching the edit; the second is WiFI sharing between smart devices and PCs. Tools like Airstash provide an excellent sharing work around.

Table 4.2 Video app features.

	iMovie	Voddio	Video Pad	Cute Cut
Two-track video	Yes	Yes	Yes	Yes
Multi-track audio	Yes 6 tracks	Yes 4 tracks	Yes 2 tracks	Yes Multi-track
Audio level	Yes	Yes	Yes	Yes
Audio Ducking	Yes Track split	Yes Keyframe	Yes Keyframe	No
Titles and Supers	Yes	Yes	Yes	Yes
Vision FX	No	Yes	Yes	Yes
Sound FX	Yes	No	Yes	No
Record Vision	Yes	Yes	Yes	
Record Narration	Yes	Yes	Yes	
Transitions	Yes	No	Yes	Yes
Detach Audio	Yes	Yes	No	No
Render Formats	Yes	Yes	Yes	Yes
Render Resolution	Yes 4 settings	Yes 5 settings	Yes 6 settings	Yes 3 Settings
iOS	Yes	Yes	Yes	Yes
Android	No	No	Yes	No
PC	Yes	No	No?	No

KineMaster Pro from NextStreaming Corp is an Android edit app that we like a lot and that will be even more useable when Version 3 ships with support for two video tracks. With drag-and-drop support around the timeline the app makes it easy to adjust elements. Its tap, swipe, drag and split features are quick to master. KineMaster Pro has onboard tools to adjust a clip's brightness, contrast and color saturation, and to rotate videos or images. Like many of the apps it includes a set of transitions, a titles tool and has multiple audio tracks. You'll need to sign up to remove the watermark. Check to make sure it is available for your Android device. Bring on Version 3.

Ivo's Tip: Use Filmic Pro 2 for advanced work, export to iMovie 2.0 or Voddio for the edit and send the finished video to YouTube or back to Camera Roll. If you need to send to an FTP server but don't want to sign up to VeriCorder's network service then export from Camera Roll to iFTP Pro (read the instructions!), or use the FILMIC Pro's free FTP transfer function.

RECHARGEABLE LIGHTS

These small battery-operated lights are essential for working quickly in low light conditions. Those that have a dimmer control are best. A smartphone cradle with a hot-shoe is essential for mounting the lights which can cost US$30–100. I prefer the Manfrotto series of LED lights that include dimming functions.

MINI TRIPOD, MONO-POD, STEADY-CAM AND MORE

Fix your mCamLite to a monopod (or a tripod) to add stability and save your arms when recording interviews. Be careful not to let the monopod restrict your movement. After all, mojo is all about being mobile. Look for a solid lightweight build. Below is a list of devices we tested.

You will need a cradle for your smart device to use the above tripods. However, we adhere to the *mojo is mobile* principle, so you need to learn to hand hold. But there are circumstances (see Chapter 5) where a tripod will be helpful. The above tripods are all good alternatives and all with different strengths. The Rode

Figure 4.11 Ivo recording a selfie standup with smartphone fixed to Manfrotto Pixi using a Shoulderpod S1.

Ivo Burum

grip not listed above is another favorite as it transforms into a tripod and a stand, and is very compact and light. The Manfrotto Pocket is very cool because it is so small, works with all smartphones, compact cameras and small DSLRs. Placed on a table, with one of its 2 cm legs articulated, it can be used to record a piece to camera in almost any situation or location. The Joby

Table 4.3 Tripod options and features.

	Manfrotto Pixi	Manfrotto Pocket	Rode Mini Tripod	Joby Micro	Hafnel C5	Manfrotto 560B-1
Extension	No	No	No	No	Yes	Yes
Articulated head	Yes	No	Yes	Yes	Yes	Yes
Lightweight	Yes	Yes	Yes	Yes	No	No
Screw	¼ and ⅜	¼	¼	No	¼	¼
Height	6"	1" (2.5 cm)	8"	3"	32–144	45–155
Tripod	Yes	Yes	Yes	Yes	Yes	Yes
Monopod	No	No	No	No	Yes	Yes

Grip Tight Micro Stand is another favorite because of its quick release and variable clamp that will suit almost any smartphone. The Manfrotto 560B-1 Monopod (US$170) is terrific for interviews as it won't mask the interviewee and its articulated arm enables lateral movement even when fixed.

Steadicam

The Smoothee is an easy-to-use Steadicam for the iPhone or Go Pro, that works. Weighing in at under half a pound the Smoothee is ideal for the extended mojo kit to provide higher production shots at an event opening.

It takes some time to calibrate out of the box, but once this is done and fine-tuned, it's just a matter of getting used to controlling the east–west axis of the frame. At US$200 it won't break the bank.

Boombandit

The Boombandit was invented by ex-grip Marcus McLeod from Australia. It is the first lightweight camera crane designed specifically for mobile phones, Go Pro and other compact cameras.

Take your camera from the ground to over three meters in the air in one graceful movement and float to where the action is. You can push the camera over the edge of a ravine, into the door of a car for motoring work or over a bubbling saucepan. Create walk and talk interviews from any angle or height from the ground to three meters.

Figure 4.12 The Steadicam Smoothee

Ivo Burum

Weighing in at just 800 grams and packing down to about two feet, you can sling it into a pack or over your back for that special shot. The next version of it will be carbon fiber. At US$230 it's the cheapest crane I've ever used, and it works.

Figure 4.13 The
Boombandit and inventor
Mark McLeod.

Courtesy Boombandit

Drones

There are a large array of drones that are used by news and
general production, to record stills or video, in circumstances that
would otherwise be cost prohibitive (requiring choppers) or geographically difficult (getting a top shot in a flat desert landscape).
Drones can be used to go where journalists can't, such as over a
live volcano crater, to record lava flow. Drones are also used by
the military.

Depending on the region in which you work a permit and some
training may be required to fly drones. As I have a restricted pilot's
license I jumped right on in and found it a blast.

Drones come in many different sizes and prices. I bought a cheap-
ish Parrott AR 2.0 (US$300). The AR 2.0 is operated via an app
on either an Android or iOS smart device. It has an onboard 1280

x 720 camera that streams video to the app controller and also includes a USB connector for when media needs to be stored on the drone. It has a terrific feature that enables users to set a height restriction (perfect when learning). The 'Rescue' button activates two propellers instead of the whole four to help shake the drone out of a tree.

Ivo's Tip: Make sure you do your research, because power to weight is critical. Generally you will need twice as much thrust as payload. So work out how heavy your camera is and plan accordingly.

Figure 4.14 Ivo piloting the AR 2.0 Drone with his smartphone.

Jo Williams

Portable Power

We use the following portable USB devices to extend battery life on our smart devices:

Mophie Juice Pack Plus or similar battery jacket almost doubles the battery life between charges. Price: US$120.

Mophie Powerstation XL (12000mAh) will charge two tablets simultaneously. Price: US$130.

Maxell Mobile Charger (5000mAh) recharges the smartphone battery up three times. Price: US$45.

Kathmandu Solar Charger will keep you shooting well into the night. Price: US$35.

LIVE STREAMING FROM SMARTPHONES

The processors used in smartphones are super-fast and with good WiFi or 3G/4G connections they can be used to stream live video. Cheap solutions like Qik (now Skype Qik) or Bambuser enable users to upload content to proprietary systems. With more powerful options like Dejero you can upload to personal servers using a number of live broadcast options.

While all advanced systems like Dejero and LiveU work slightly differently, they manage bandwidth and latency across 3G, 4G and WiFi connections by effectively splitting the signal and sending it across multiple connections, before bonding, or re-encoding it, at the destination. The systems are costly and can include monthly fees. But you transmit in high definition live (1.5 second latency) with talk back (IFB) support when using an iOS device.

HYBRID SYSTEMS AND SHARING FACILITIES

As mentioned earlier in this chapter mojo is as much about skills and application as it is about technology. In some instances it may be beneficial to shoot on a DSLR (DSLM) or video camera. A hybrid approach will facilitate specific outcomes – the use of powerful lenses, specific apertures or shutter speeds, or automatic and more advanced zooms.

I have used the above DSLR or DSLM cameras and while they are all ideal for mojo work, the advantage of the Lumix GH4 is the quality of the video, which can be recorded at 200Mbps and even at 4K. The other advantage of the GH4 is cost. Much cheaper than the alternatives, the Lumix system offers a large series of journalism lenses including the 12–35 f/2.8 (equivalent to 24–70) or 35–100 f/2.8 (equivalent to 70–200), at a fraction of the cost of other leading brands.

If your job requires full on video journalism functionality for very busy documentary shooting, my choice is the Sony PXW-X70 video camera. Very compact, with a one-inch chip, this ready for 4K camera shoots at 50Mbps, includes two XLR audio inputs and functions extremely well in low light.

Ivo's Tip: The advantage of DSLRs is the ability to control the depth of field. A shallow depth of field can also be a disadvantage when shooting video.

TRANSFER DEVICES

Mojos in the field will need to share their media across devices or platforms so that more than one journalist can use it or when media is augmented in post-production. For example, if a still image or video is captured on a camera app it can be exported to Camera Roll then to a control app like Video Grade (or Snapseed for stills) where it is graded. Then it's sent back to Camera Roll and on to the edit app of choice. In particular DSLR or DSLM media (stills or video) may need to be transferred to a PC or smart device for more advanced editing and post-production.

The above example is an app-to-app transfer that's generally an onboard move. To shift media quickly between devices or platforms for editing or storage use a transfer device like Airstash, SanDisk Connect Wireless Media Drive, SanDisk Wireless Flash or the Kingston MobileLite.

WiFi Transfer devices establish a local WiFi network between the media drive and your smart device in order to stream up to five sources simultaneously. Switch on the media drive, activate the drive's proprietary app on your smart device, choose the media drive in your WiFi settings and follow prompts to share the content back and forth.

We have tested these four media transfer devices.

Airstash   SanDisk Wireless Media Drive

Figure 4.15 WiFi transfer devices make moving media across devices and platforms a breeze. They also act as storage bins for media when working on location.

Courtesy Maxell and SanDisk

Airstash by Maxell (US$80) and the *Connect Wireless Media Drive* (US$119) by SanDisk are two of the most useful. Both devices use an SD card with the SanDisk capable of storing a whopping 128GB. The SanDisk has the advantage of shipping with 64GB of on-board memory. They will run for seven hours plus and stream to multiple devices simultaneously.

A cheaper option using a Micro SD card and offering four hours of battery life is the *SanDisk Connect Wireless Flash Drive* (US$80). The *Kingston Mobile Lite Wireless* (US$50) drive has up to five hours of battery life and can use 128GB SD cards; it also acts as an emergency battery for mobile devices. All devices require a free app (Android or iOS) and all transfer a variety of content and media across devices and platforms. Depending on the level of memory you require, the above devices can cost from US$50 to US$200.

Voddio WiFi is an iOS to iOS media exchange protocol via local WiFi (enabled when the once-only fee is paid that unlocks sharing). This feature allows the user to select one device as a server, the other a browser and share from server to browser; or to input the device's IP address into a computer's search bar, to view or download the device's files on the computer.

Using Air Drop, iOS devices (iPhone 5 and 6, fifth generation iPod touch or newer, an iPad mini, fourth generation iPad or newer) using iOS 8 can Air Drop files between devices. Air Drop uses Bluetooth to create a peer to peer WiFi network. Once Air Drop is activated on both devices, it's simply a matter of selecting media, tapping the share panel and following the prompts. You'll be asked to accept or decline the transfer.

A number of third-party apps are available to share media between PC and iOS devices. We've found *Air Sharing* useful. It works on iOS devices running 5.1 or later and transforms your device into a virtual hard drive.

ADAPTORS AND LENSES

Adaptors and lenses are available or being developed that transform the iPhone into a pseudo DSLR. The Photojojo lens adapter enables manual use of Canon or Nikon DSLR lenses. The Artefact Group in the USA is developing a wireless viewfinder interchangeable lens (WVIL) version with the processing power of more expensive larger DSLRs. The group's aim is to produce adapters for Nikon, Canon and other lenses.

Sony has introduced the pocket-sized QX10 and QX100 lens cameras that sit on the front of an iPhone or Android device and are controlled remotely through an app on the device. On offer is a better 20 Mega Pixel camera, with a 10x zoom and ISO range up to 25600.

The future might see hybrid concepts like Black Design's i9 that potentially marries the Leica M9 camera front with an iPhone back. The iPhone is anticipated to dock into the camera and replace the film role or the SD card.

Below is an example of Burum Media's advanced mojo kit:

1. **Manfrotto 560B Monopod**
2. **mCamLite**
3. **iRig HD Mic**
4. **Manfrotto 360 Led**
5. **Sennheiser MKE400**
6. **Rode Smart Lav +**
7. **Sony UWP D11 Radio Mics**
8. **Air Stash WiFi USB Tranfer**
9. **Mophie PowerStation XL**
10. **Lowepro Classic 100**

Figure 4.16 The above list includes a number of levels and shows that developing a mojo kit can become expensive depending on the level of gear and the type of smartphone.

Rode, Maxell, Action Life Media, Sony, Senheiserr

Here's my favorite small and cheap mojo kit:

1. Shoulder Pod S1 (US$35)
2. Manfotto Pixi (US$25) (also works as a short magic arm), or you can use a Rode Mic Stand (US$30)
3. Mini Mic (US$25)
4. Digital Led Light (US$40)

Just over US$100 plus the cost of your choice of smartphone gets you an effective mojo kit.

In closing, multimedia journalism sounds very technical and having the right tools is always important no matter whether you are a dentist, a panel beater, or a mojo. But mojo is more about empowering individuals with the skills to create their own voice – about linking community with a global communication sphere. As such it's about empowering people with skills and a process that enables and encourages participants to have and express their own views. Hence real mojo, the type described in this book, requires a journalistic and multimedia skill set to realize the true potential of the technology, which is what we discuss in the following chapters.

CHAPTER 5

COMPOSING VISUAL PROOF ON SMARTPHONES

Ivo Burum

SUMMARY

Multimedia or mojo storytelling creates raw user-generated content (UGC) for news outlets; and feature-type user-generated stories (UGS) for online, paywall and web TV formats. Whether it's creating UGC or UGS, mojos need to know how to capture and compose powerful images quickly. To do this mojos need to know which images will tell their story best. In this chapter we introduce a few basic concepts and techniques for recording visual media in the field. I discuss how to work on location to best cover an event and I introduce the concept of shooting to edit on a mobile.

In the early 1990s I began experimenting with self-shot television formats for television. More complex to shoot than video diaries, self-shot series need to be formatted so they can be replicated like any TV series. The self-shot style was a manifestation of what Michael Rosenblum and others had been calling video journalism since the 1960s. These formats were a forerunner to the UGC forms of today; the big difference now is anyone has the tools to shoot, edit and publish their own content, stories and programs.

As the self-shot or video journalist (VJ) style developed and became more popular it found a home on prime-time current affairs programs. Younger journalists wanting to make a name for themselves, or camera people and citizens wanting to do journalism, embraced VJ.

From 1995, the Internet became readily available and a relatively free and limitless publication platform was born. In 2005, smartphones transformed a PC generation into users of intimate hand-held devices. Two years later the iPhone and third-party apps transformed the mobile revolution into a hugely lucrative industry. As technology became smaller it seemed to get more powerful. Driven by investment in the app industry, smartphones transformed into powerful creative suites able to capture, edit and publish high-quality video and audio.

Smartphones spawned a new group of citizen content producers who found the technology addictive and the lure of ready-made publishing platforms like YouTube irresistible. Mixed with an already rampant voyeuristic culture, born from years of reality and self-shot TV programs, Internet accessibility led to an exponential increase in UGC production. In 2015 citizens uploaded a staggering 157 million hours of video – enough to fill 18000 channels 24/7 for a year. Essentially my mojo workshops were driven by the real fear that the potential of the smartphone, as a professional politicized content creation tool, would never be realized.

I have been teaching citizens to shoot their own content for television series for almost 30 years. My mojo workshops are heavily influenced by a neo-journalistic approach that relies on wrapping new technologies and workflows in relevant legacy skills. My background as a journalist, executive producer and writer on many TV series, including nightly public affairs, influences my view about mojo praxis in fast turn-around production. My work as a cameraperson, journalist and producer on international current affairs shows – where we were often called on to multi-skill – informs my view about the importance of the holistic nature of mojo production. Today a mojo is able to shoot, write, edit, record narration, mix audio, grade footage and upload the revised and finished video from remote locations, without ever stepping into an edit suite.

Hence the information in this chapter, about working in the field, is based on lessons I learned from working as a producer and journalist in remote international locations, where a more holistic skills set is required. It is also based on self-shot workshops I have run in television and mojo workshops with students, citizens and with print journalists at a number of Asian, European and Australian media houses.

CHOOSING THE RIGHT MOJO EQUIPMENT

The mobile has become so smart that users, those futurists Howard Rheingold called "smart mobs" (2002), need to smarten and become *net smart*. Being a net-smart mojo means planning what you want to record, knowing how to record it and having the right equipment for the job. Mojo is an all-inclusive form of multimedia storytelling that combines journalism, videography, photography, writing, editing and publishing from a hand-held smart device. We use iPhones for most of our mojo work. However as most of the information included in this book relates to ways of working it will apply to mojos using any form of smartphone, DSLR or video camera.

Ivo's Tip: Thinking about story first and then technology will help you choose the right gear for your mojo job.

The first thing I'd like to suggest is that your story, schedule and your intended result, might define your shooting style and the level and type of mojo that's required. For example, shooting sports, or wildlife, may require long lenses and a DSLR or video camera in addition to your smartphone. In some cases mojos might use adapters on their smartphone cradle and attach a DSLR lens for added range, depth of field and control over exposure. Once shot, media on the video camera or DSLR will be transferred to a laptop or smart device for editing. The point is that technology is not the answer to everything and a focus on story can help determine a level of technology.

In this book we take an approach to mojo that does not throw the baby out with the bathwater and retains important legacy skills. Some of the messages and skills may be familiar to you. But here they are in a mojo context.

BE PREPARED AND BE PROFESSIONAL

The first important thing to understand when working as a mojo is that you can be as professional as network crews if you prepare well and know your craft. Mojos need to be ready for all eventualities and the best way to make time slow down on a breaking news story, is to have all bases covered. I know you'll be thinking: How can we cover all bases on a breaking news story? You can by thinking in advance about the story (theme and characters), knowing your gear and knowing the limitations of the location. If it's a rush job then you need to get the preparation done en route in the car, on the train, or in the plane, and well before you get to location.

Ivo's Tip: Treat every shoot as if it's an overseas shoot – there is no going back for more. The best way to do this is to prepare and then prepare some more.

You will need to research your story – even breaking news items benefit from research:

- **Do you have a five-point plan?**
- **Do you have experts in mind to interview, and will they all be at one location?**
- **Have you thought of a lead?**

- **Have you checked the Internet for the latest on the topic or event?**
- **Do you have archive media in mind and if so how much will it cost and how will you get it?**
- **Will you need to stay overnight and can other interviewees be recorded en route?**
- **How will you upload your media?**

A FIVE-POINT PLAN

All stories will have a beginning, middle and an end. Once we begin to understand a story we realize there are a number of additional arc points. The five- to seven-point plan is made before the shoot and adjusted accordingly as elements develop during the shoot and the edit.

Figure 5.1 A five-point arc is a basic structure for a UGS plan that is effective for keeping developing stories and keeping them focused in the field.

Ivo Burum

A plan is not prescriptive or restrictive and helps maintain focus when mojos become inundated with the weight of creativity and when it all gets frantic. While working on difficult location-based current affairs series, like ABCs *Foreign Correspondent*, I always had a rough story plan written on one of those tiny yellow notepads, the type that fits into a pocket.

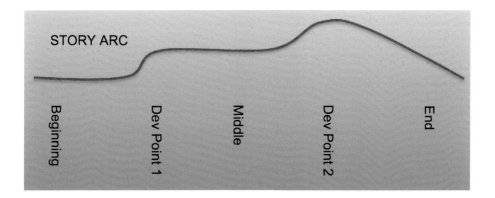

Once you know the story this pre-record checklist might help:

- **Is the smartphone charged and did you bring the car adapter, solar charger or battery pack so that it can be recharged?**
- **Have you switched to Airplane Mode (in Settings) to stop calls and WiFi interference?**
- **Will shooting in a dense location such as a jungle require a portable light?**
- **Do you have the right microphones and batteries?**
- **Do you have a camera cradle and can you carry a tripod or monopod?**
- **Will the onboard camera app be sufficient or will the location and the job require a more advanced app like Filmic Pro?**
- **Does the job require a hybrid mojo approach and use of a DSLR and various lenses? If so:**
  - **Do you have an Airstash or another device to use to transfer media onto or off your smart device or laptop?**
- **Will the edit be done on location and if so:**
  - **Do you have the right edit app and is there enough power to complete the edit?**
  - **Will there be 3G/4G or WiFi connectivity to enable story upload?**
- **Does someone know where you will be working and have you developed an exit strategy?**

Once research is complete and you are happy that you understand the technical imperatives, you'll need to investigate SCRAP – Story, Character, Resolution, Actuality and Production. SCRAP is a story tool that can help mojos develop the elements in a multi-planar mojo story. SCRAP is a modular tool, just like Lego, that enables mojos to try various combinations of story elements. SCRAP is a key to developing and preparing mojo UGS story plans, and is discussed at length in Chapter 7.

BASIC SMARTPHONE HANDLING

One aspect of being a good mojo journalist is being prepared to respond immediately to breaking news. At one level this means knowing how to use gear effectively. You will never be able to manage the adrenalin of working on breaking news, or in a war zone, unless you practice using your equipment beforehand.

Don't try to suppress the adrenalin, learn to manage and control it. Stressors only turn into stress when we can't affect a result. The release of stress hormones activate fight/flight and freezing responses – and our brain goes into overload and we are unable to manage inputs. The best way to learn to deal with the stress of fast news production is to practice. Get out in your community and capture local events as they unfold. Try to work with the bustle of the crowd and record process action (like a wood turner working) that can't be stopped framing quickly and shooting the actuality before actions or events stop.

Ivo's Tip: When you are working on location always carry what you need. The smartphone should be at the ready with a microphone attached. I usually plug in a small shotgun microphone that uses camera power, so that I can't forget to switch it on. The remaining gear should fit into a small backpack or a bum bag sitting below the stomach, but above the crotch, so that you can run easily.

HAND HELD OR TRIPOD?

Your choice as to whether you shoot hand held or on a tripod can determine how dynamic your footage will look. Using a tripod and shooting from a distance on long lenses gives footage a spy look and that's not really what journalism and multimedia storytelling is about. It also puts the camera and the microphone a long way from the audio source and the action. Without access you'll end up with weak location actuality and muddy audio.

Great journalism is partly synonymous with good access – if you are not close enough you may as well not be there. The better the access at an accident, in the fray with water police as they dredge a river, or with fire fighters outside a burning building, the more unique the material. If you have access the tripod or long lens will not be necessary and your standard smartphone will do the job. The wider lens that ships with some cradles will make your smartphone even more useful.

While some journalists advocate using a tripod even in situations where hand held is required, my advice is resist and get in close on a wide lens. The weight of a smartphone cradle, like the aluminum-bodied mCamLite, will help steady your shot and by being close you will feel the story. Only use a tripod when it's absolutely essential, when recording that super-wide establishing shot of the Rift Valley, or that long lens shot of a person drowning in the middle of a river. Being close to action and shooting without a tripod, puts you in a flowing state of body and mind, where you feel the unfolding story and are able to move with it to cover developing actuality.

Here are a few tips for working hand held:

- **Rest your body on a wall, or your elbows on a table, or on the front of your car to create stability.**
- **If the smartphone is in a cradle it will probably be able to support itself on a table. But is that what you want — to leave the camera stationary? Probably *yes* for a sit down interview and *no* when you cover unfolding actuality.**

- **If you pull your elbows close to your body you will create a strong triangle with the camera to support the shot. But bear in mind that it's hard walking like that. Try it and you'll see that you look and feel like a Dalek in a straitjacket.**
- **Bend your elbows and knees to feel the center of your weight and when panning the camera left and right, pivot your body, not your hands.**

Mojo is really about being mobile and this means being in amongst unfolding actuality; so move in close to get a variety of shots rather than sitting back on a tripod relying on your zoom. Most smart-phone zooms are digital and while they should be used if required, you will do better to track in and shoot close on the wide end of your lens, because:

- **The shot is steady;**
- **The subject is audible;**
- **You're close to evolving actuality and will feel the emotion.**

Ivo's Tip: Always check your location to see where the actuality is, where interviewees are and where your escape route is.

Now that we know how to dance with the smartphone, we need to understand the detail of what we are filming and how to cover a sequence.

COVERAGE

How a camera is used and what shots are chosen will partly determine the style of a story. An action-packed news story might require a lot of useable short shots with driving narration and choice factual and emotive sync grabs. A slower-paced short feature might require more in-depth interviews with supporting B roll that captures emotive and reflective moments. The degree to which you set a style in the field will impact the level of creative and editorial complexity during the edit.

Shots or Sequences

Shooting a sequence is when you record a number of shots that relate to each other to tell a narrative or story. Follow the action and move from one shot to the next varying the frame size so that shots are different enough and can be edited easily. For example, if you are filming football training the sequence might include: a wide shot (WS) showing where the game is and who's training, some tighter mid-shots showing the contact and some close-up (CU) shots showing the pain and the ecstasy. You might call a sequence like this 'training B roll'. This will remind you that this clip or sequence contains a number of different shots to cover a training montage.

Thinking in terms of sequence gives you more effective shots. This five-shot rule is often discussed:

- *Hands*: **doing something shows what's being done and is often very textural, and if close enough can be very emotive**
- *Face*: **shows who is doing it and can show the pain or the ecstasy associated with the activity.**
- *Two shot*: **shows a relationship between the hands, face and activity so the closer shots are not disembodied. This shot can be run at any point of the edit.**

- *Over the shoulder*: this is a tricky shot as the framing needs to be right and for video this requires some practice and height. It is a confronting relational shot. It is often a great shot when you can stand on a chair and use the long end of the zoom to pack the frame between head and hands especially if you have aperture control to create a shallow depth of field.
- *The special shot*: I generally love this the best either when I'm shooting or when I ask a camera person to bring me back a couple of their special shots. This type of shot is generally unplanned and is discovered on location in the course of filming.

While the five shots mentioned above are generally present in each well-shot sequence, when covering unfolding actuality such as a car accident things happen so fast that you'd miss the actuality if you buttoned off and waited to set up each shot. So it's nearly always best to think of those shots as a sequence – one following the other–that experienced mojos can almost edit in their head and in camera.

The "How to Cover a Scene" video at the link www.focalpress.com/cw/burum describes how to sequence a 30-second video. The example shows how a three-shot sequence is used to cover a scene and demonstrates that recording the shots without stopping the activity saves time, increases the number of available shots and doesn't impede the actuality.

Figure 5.2 shows that if you shoot and save a CU of someone playing with an iPhone, then a CU of the person's face, and finally a wider relational shot showing the person doing the activity, you would have three shots that tell a story – *who's* doing it, *what* they're doing and *where*. If you shot the three shots as a sequence, without stopping between each shot, you'd end up with *three extra shots* and you will have covered the unfolding story without wasting precious time stopping and starting.

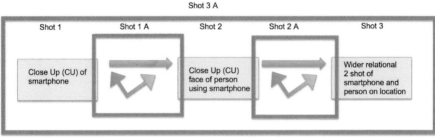

Shot 3 A

Shot 1 — Shot 1 A — Shot 2 — Shot 2 A — Shot 3

Close Up (CU) of smartphone

Close Up (CU) face of person using smartphone

Wider relational 2 shot of smartphone and person on location

Shot 1A: Use a short piece of Shot 1, tilt up to the face and use the move and short piece of Shot 2

Shot 2A: Use a short piece of Shot 2 and move out to Shot 3

Shot 3A: Move from Shot 1 to 2 and to 3 all in one move

Figure 5.2 Sequencing shots.

Ivo Burum

The Devil is in the Detail

Let's look at how we might shoot a sequence of someone pulling up to a house on a bicycle. The sequence could be shot in three shots, or it might consist of the following shots: wide shot riding up to gate and stopping, mid-shot getting off the bicycle, a shot of the gate opening, a wider shot wheeling the bicycle into the yard, a close-up of putting the bicycle on its stand, taking off the bicycle gloves and helmet, closing the gate, walking to the front door. Every little detail might be important. But ask yourself – how much coverage do I need in a news story?

Both versions – one with basic coverage with narration and one with the variety of shots described above – are shown in this video: www.focalpress.com/cw/burum. See which one you like best. Is there a difference to the feeling and the dynamics of the sequence?

Tom Gelai, an experienced network cameraman who works across news/media genres, says: "It's all about story and not about genre. If you feel the story the coverage and the style will come." Strong coverage is about having the right elements (actuality, B roll, narration, piece-to-camera or stand-up, interviews, graphics and music are discussed in Chapter 7) or visual proof to enable the story to be edited with all its gravitas – news worthiness, drama, emotion, action and dynamics.

Ivo's Tip: Sequencing doesn't mean getting stuck in an observational mode. You can still ask the subject to repeat a quick sound bite. The aim of sequencing is to focus on the story and the edit while on location, which is important for mojos who generally edit in the field.

When recording story elements consider the following.

FRAMING

When hand holding, make sure you are comfortable by bending your knees. Dance with the camera and choose the frame that best demonstrates what you are trying to say and show. Here are some basic frame sizes and how they might be used:

- **Extreme wide shot (EWS): The subject can just be seen but it shows the area of the shoot.**

Figure 5.3 Standard frame sizes.

Ivo Burum

- **Wide shot (WS): The height of the subject is seen clearly and we see the surroundings and background in a story context.**

Figure 5.4 **Standard frame sizes.**

Ivo Burum

- **Mid-shot (MS): This shows the subject in detail while also showing some background. This is often used in a piece to camera (PTC) shot on location, with the subject off center to show the unfolding actuality in the background.**

Figure 5.5 **Standard frame sizes.**

Ivo Burum

- **Medium close-up (MCU): This is the most used shot in news because it is emotive and also wide enough to see some of the actuality in the background. This is often used in an interview and is intercut with a MS and a CU.**

Figure 5.6 Standard frame sizes.

Ivo Burum

- **Close-up (CU): This is used to convey extreme detail and emotion. Use the wide-angle lens and move the camera closer to the subject. A zoomed shot will highlight any movement by the camera operator and make the shot appear shaky.**

Figure 5.7 Standard frame sizes.

Ivo Burum

Be careful not to waste space in your frame by having too much headroom or empty foreground. The rule of thirds suggests an image is more pleasing when divided in three imaginary vertical and horizontal zones. The aim is to balance the elements in the image. For example, when you record a PTC you might move to one side of the frame and balance the other with relevant story content.

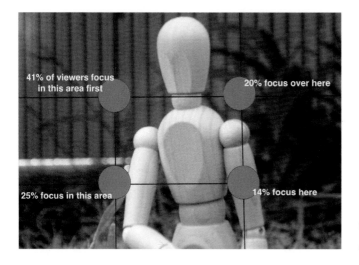

Figure 5.8 Rule of thirds.

Ivo Burum

When shooting overlay or B roll you might try changing the camera position, not just the shot size. Give yourself options for the edit by making sure you have too much B roll.

FOR HOW LONG DO I HOLD SHOTS?

One of the most common mistakes people who have just picked up a camera make is that they don't hold their shots for long enough or zoom in and out perpetually. Even though as little as 18 frames of a shot might be useful, it's important to hold shots for at least ten seconds.

***Ivo's Tip: If I am working fast I concentrate on
getting useable information and not shots.***

While every picture is worth a thousand words, I only consider it useable when it relates to my story. It's pointless having a thousand words if they aren't relevant. Always ask: What's happening in the frame? Of course, shoot special shots, but make sure you cover your story structure with useable story specific shots.

So what's useable? The more time you spend in the edit suite the more you'll know about what works, and what not to shoot. When you are more experienced you will learn how to use as little as three-quarters of a second of a shot. If you are sequencing you might cover a whole action – all five shots (described above) and then some, without buttoning off (switching off). One advantage of holding a shot for an extended time, perhaps for 45 seconds or longer, is that you are rolling if something unexpected happens. If these long shots are interesting, we call them *tea ceremonies* – where even the most basic movement can be a work of art. Named after a Japanese tea ceremony this type of shot or sequence can include pensive close-ups, slow elegant movements, emotive looks and telling hand gestures. Hence, team ceremony shots are very useful for running with poignant narration. But surely, I hear you say, there is no tea ceremony at the scene of an accident.

How could you use the tea ceremony shot or concept at the scene of an accident?

DYNAMIC CAMERA MOVEMENT

Movement is shown in two ways: subject within a frame, or by moving the camera and the frame. Camera movement within a frame means the frame remains static and is filled with dynamic actuality. Movement around the frame suggests following dynamic actuality.

You might consider the following:

- *Follow shot*: **Anticipate action by trying to predict where the subject/action will go, and be ready to shoot action when the subject moves into frame. Think ahead and get positioned ready to anticipate the action and follow the subject.**
- *Static frame*: **Let action happen within the frame and don't constantly move the camera in a futile attempt to cover everything. But don't be afraid to whip the camera around if something happens. You can always edit the whip pan out, if you don't want it.**
- *Walk out*: **Allow your subject to move out of frame, rather than trying to follow them with your camera. If you follow the person keeping them in frame before cutting to a different shot of them sitting down, it can create a mental disconnect. The viewer wonders how that person got from walking to sitting (from one frame to the next). However, if they are seen walking out of frame in the first shot, then it's logical to the viewer that the person would be seen walking into or sitting in another shot.**

Types of movements using the camera are:

- *Pan*: **is a horizontal movement left or right and is used to establish wide shots or to cover a group of people or objects.**

- *Tilt*: is an up or down motion used to cover something tall like a building, or to follow a person from a standing position to a kneeling or sitting position.
- *Track*: is where the camera follows or moves alongside the person or object; it's used when the subject is moving from one place to another and often during a PTC.

SCREEN DIRECTION

The term "crossing the line" is a traditional phrase based on an imaginary line between two people who may be talking to each other – one talking left to right and the other right to left. In our example below: Person B, covered by Camera 1, is talking right to left (from right of frame to left of frame); Person A on Camera 2 is talking left to right. Each time we cut to either of these people we know who they are talking to because their screen direction – right to left and left to right – remains constant. Once a camera crosses the imaginary line, and films one of the people talking the other they will be talking the wrong way. In our example when Camera 3 crosses the line to record Person B talking to Person A, Person B is now talking left to right, the same screen direction of Person A. This is as if Person B has moved to the other Person A's position and its called crossing the line.

In providing the above example I'm not suggesting you shouldn't cross the line. Go for it, cross as often as you like, but learn how to cross the line. Once you know about the line you'll learn how to cross it and cheat screen direction. In Australian rules football, the boundary rider, a roving reporter and camera person, with a ground-level neutral-type perspective, is used to help directors make line crosses by finding shots with a completely different perspective. The reality is that audiences expect a line cross, but the trick is to learn to make them seamless.

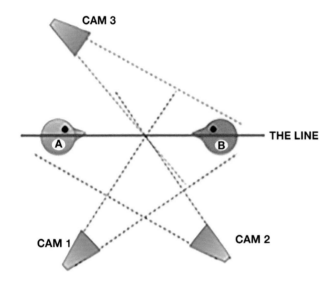

Figure 5.9 **Screen direction.**

Ivo Burum

Ivo's Tip: One simple way around a line cross is to cut to a neutral close-up.

LIGHTING

Getting the subject to look right on camera (exposure and framing) while working quickly is all about sensing the light. Former multi-award-winning ABC *Foreign Correspondent* and *Four Corners* cinematographer Wayne Harley says it's about understanding and playing with planes of light: "We don't notice this usually but it's the job of the camera man to see and feel the light and use it quickly" (1999). Working in news and current affairs journalism is about reacting to the moment, and understanding and using natural light is often the key to getting a useable shot. The value of light is the degree to which it illuminates the subject. Sensing your light or knowing where it's coming from (behind, in front or from the side) and what it's doing (flat, appearing, disappearing) is a first step to successful lighting.

Outdoor Light

Outdoor light is difficult to work with because it's not timeless and hence is rarely controlled. One minute it's bright and warm the next cloudy and cool. The best outdoor light occurs in the early morning or at dusk, which is often referred to as the "golden" or "magic hour." This is a favorite time for cinematographers. But when shooting news you are not always going to have the luxury of choosing your lighting moment. So I have the following tips for shooting in outdoor light:

- **Avoid high noon if you can and try to film the subject so that the light is in front of them (behind your shoulders) and not behind the subject (see Figure 5.10) as this will help exposure.**
- **Each light source has its own power and at dusk and dawn the light is warmer (more golden) and shadows are softer than during the middle of the day. The middle of the day is a time of high contrast. Images are sharp and defined and colors are saturated.**
- **At night try to use natural light sources like the moon, fires, flashlights, candles, car headlights or your portable light.**

Indoor Light

For day interiors if possible use natural light like the sun through a window and/or available light sources such as desk lamps, ceiling lights or your portable light. If you find the right natural light you need to work fast before you lose it.

Here are some tips for shooting with light:

- **Low light means muddy or grainy pictures. So add light – lamps, street lamp, a full moon, on-camera portable lights (but stay clear of those with large batteries as they will unbalance the camera).**
- **If more control over the shot is required you might use a DSLR with a bigger chip and changeable lenses. A wider aperture (low number) on a DSLR means you will have a shallow depth of field, which is great for moody scenes and static interviews, but not necessarily for news or documentary video footage. The same shallow depth of field that makes DSLRs effective when recording interviews can make them a nightmare to work with when shooting evolving actuality, where you need extended depth of field.**

Figure 5.10 **Direction of light.**

Ivo Burum

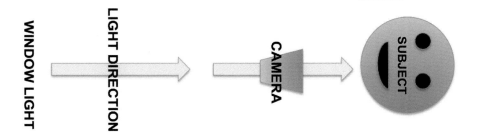

Back Light

Sometimes you want a silhouette effect. Having your subject back lit by a light or sitting in front of a bright window are just two ways. If you do need to sit your subject in front of a window so that you have to point your camera into the light, but don't want them to be back lit, you will need to move in close, lock exposure on your subject, then move back to re-frame the shot. This will result in a blown-out (over-exposed) window and a correctly exposed subject. Another option would be to compensate with some fill light on your subject. The best option is to turn your subject around and place your camera between them and the light source, as shown in the above diagram.

Fill Light

Fill light is used to balance the background and foreground exposure. A portable LED light sitting on your camera lighting your subject can often balance the exposure between exterior (background) and interior (fill). If your light has a dimmer switch you can use it to fine tune the balance between inside and outside exposure. You might also have a color temperature switch to select between indoor (warmer 2500 to 3600 degrees Kelvin) and outdoor (cooler 5600 degrees Kelvin and above) temperatures.

Wayne Harley is an award-winning news and current affairs cameraman, a former executive producer of ABC Foreign Correspondent and a Four Corners producer. Here are his five tips for a mojo in exotic locations:

1. Have two cameras, your smartphone and something like a Panasonic GH4 – you can happily film away with either in a lot of places (like airports) and no one will say a thing. Don't underestimate how powerful a good quality still can be.
2. Always have a medical kit, at the very least something for your gut to kill off the bugs. Water sterilizer pills

– especially if you're heading into central or northern Africa. A bandage of some sort.

3. A small tripod like a Miller and don't skint on the head. Would you put re-treads on a Ferrari! And get yourself one of those Gorilla-Pod tripods.

4. Garbage bags – for your dirty laundry or instant weather cover for your gear and don't underestimate what sand and wind can do to your equipment. Sealable plastic sandwich bags – put your receipts in, 'cause sure as hell you're going to lose them otherwise.

5. Maximum size carry-on suitcase (with wheels) to carry your cameras, lenses and batteries on to the plane. That's a lot of weight, and if you've ever come through Heathrow, you'll know it's a long, long, walk.

LOCATION AUDIO

We devote Chapter 6 to recording location audio and we discuss recording techniques and a variety of microphone options. In Chapter 8 we discuss how to conduct and record interview audio, and in Chapter 10 we briefly introduce the concept of audio post-production. The current discussion around smartphone audio is all about multi-track. Most smartphones only have one audio input. Even if you use a splitter and two audio sources, or if you record onto a multi-track app, you'll still have one audio file. One dual audio workflow – resulting in two audio files – is to record one source on the smartphone and the other on a digital recorder like a Zoom H1 or H5. This way you will have two audio files. Finally, the best advice I can provide about how to record clean audio is what I was told as a young journalist – put the microphone as close as possible to the sound source, your subject.

In closing, after technical and creative, one of the main variables in UGS production is the strength of interviewees. Look for great talent, talkers who are willing to share their story and then make the interview interesting. How you choose to record them will impact how interviewees sound and feel. Will it be a sit-down style or will it be walk and talk? You might experiment and practice with different shot types to see the effect of different combinations on your interview.

Once you have mastered the technical and creative aspects of mojo and have a strong interview, recording relevant B roll will be the key to editing out superfluous dialogue and creating a dynamic UGS.

Irrespective of the level of mojo equipment used the following checklist will assist in recording strong visuals with a smartphone:

1. **To tell the story we need to shoot the story.**
2. **Plan and schedule the story to allow for all eventualities.**
3. **Switch the smartphone to airplane mode or turn off WiFi.**
4. **Shoot in the landscape or horizontal frame.**
5. **Avoid high contrast in lighting situations and shoot with the sun to your back.**
6. **Avoid shots of areas that have high contrast such as dark versus light settings, or bright sunlight and shadows.**
7. **Always wait for the numbers to start scrolling after pressing record and before you move the camera to lock the gyro into the desired frame.**
8. **Start your story with dynamic CUs or a beautiful WS establisher.**
9. **A change of angle is as good as a second unit.**
10. **To ensure that you have enough useable coverage hold your shots for at least ten seconds and even longer for tea ceremony shots.**
11. **Use B roll to shorten long sequences.**
12. **Always be on the look-out for scene opening and closing interview grabs and shots.**

13. Don't use a tripod unless necessary as it impedes mobility and interaction.

14. Don't be afraid to cross the line, but learn how to do it seamlessly using neutral shots.

15. Make sure you leave the right amount of headroom or chin room. Don't use a shot where there's excessive empty space above a person's head or too little space under their chin, because the name super might cover their mouth.

16. Depth of field is a concept that describes focus points in a frame and is often controlled by altering F-stops on a lens. On a smartphone use your focus lock to create a sense of depth in the frame, or set the subject to one side of frame to create depth in the frame beyond the subject, or make sure the frame is well lit to create sharper images through the depth of the frame. Also remember that a wide-angle shot will provide a much better depth of field than a telephoto shot zoomed in on your subject.

17. Keep quiet while shooting.

Mojos are inquisitive people who are able to capture their curiosity on a smartphone then edit and publish the images in a UGS while still at location. A good mojo is well prepared and knows the limits of their equipment. If required s/he is willing to choose one of the hybrid options discussed in Chapter 4, to make sure their visuals are exiting. But unless we hear what's being said we will only get half the story and will lose our audience. Sound recording is a refined art and is the topic of our next chapter.

REFERENCES

Harley, Wayne. 1999. Interview. Melbourne.

Keen, Andrew. 2006. *The Cult of the Amateur: User Generated Media Are Killing Our Culture and Economy*. 5th ed. London: Nicholas Brealey.

Rheingold, Howard. 2002. *Smart Mobs*. Cambridge, MA: Perseus Books.

CHAPTER 6

RECORDING LOCATION SOUND USING A SMARTPHONE

Ivo Burum

SUMMARY

Recording clean useable sound on location is an art requiring practice and the right equipment. While basic sound-recording principles remain constant, a mojo needs to know how to shoot video and record sound at the same time. In this chapter we'll explore basic sound-recording principles and the differences between microphones. I'll introduce the various cables and accessories available for recording sound with a smartphone and briefly discuss a number of apps for recording and transferring audio.

We begin hearing sounds at about 16 weeks while we are still in the womb and even before we can see. Parents' voices, intonation and rhythms can be heard above the sounds of the natural world. Today we are bombarded with noise and our senses filter out sounds that we hear but don't want to listen to. Listening and filtering out noise is a key aspect of recording clean audio. MTV has taught us that we are happy to watch the flashing over-lit shot, the whip pan or the blurry close-up, and that we like our audio clean. The key to recording useable clean audio is using the right equipment, microphone placement, access and monitoring.

Figure 6.1 Student mojo Ryan Hyde using Senheisser MKE400 shotgun microphone with smartphone and Phocus cradle.

Ivo Burum

Walter Murch, the famous Hollywood feature-film sound editor and mixer, reminds us that: "The most important thing students must learn is 90 percent of film is sound. The picture is far less important" (cited in AFTRS 2014).

While it's important never to come home without the video, Murch is right about the importance of sound in factual location-based recording. Unlike feature films and some large documentaries, which use post-synced sound and dialogue, a mojo needs to know how to record clean usable audio in the field, often in noisy locations.

A decade ago it was much simpler because, ironically, everything was more complex. You either knew what you were doing or you hired a professional sound recordist. Today mojos have to record audio without a sound recordist and edit sound without an editor. Therefore mojos need to know the basic principles of sound recording: which microphone is best and where to place it. They also need to understand the extent to which being a one-man band will compromise their ability to record audio.

For a mojo, as with any journalist working in radio, television, or online, recording location dialogue correctly is vital because the location dialogue is often the only dialogue a factual project will have. The key to recording clean dialogue is technique. The second most important aspect is the microphone. Finally, none of this is relevant without access.

LOCATION SOUND-RECORDING TECHNIQUE

The word location has a number of connotations when used to describe sound recording. In the first instance it has a topographical meaning that suggests you are not in a studio. But it also describes the proximity of the subject to the reporter, suggesting they are both in the same location. This presupposes an ability to

Figure 6.2 Mojos recording an interview on location.

Ivo Burum

communicate directly and to feel the full spectrum and emotional weight of the auditory experience in the way that watching silent pictures never does. So an important rule of recording location sound is *get in close so that you can feel the sound*; I would add so that you can *see the sound*. If you are in amongst the action you'll record more dynamic location sound, because you will *feel the scene developing* before you. You will see the activity that causes sound to happen and record the result, which is emotion and drama.

Professional boom operators are used to record sound because there is a need to drop the microphone in close to the sound source without being in shot. Even though the boom pole might be extended up to 18 feet, the microphone will sit as close as possible to the edge of frame and the subject. A mojo will probably not use a boom so s/he needs to be close to the subject and not in frame. It's important not to make the mistake of zooming in for audio. Being on the long end of the lens (the zoom) results in grainy, shaky pictures and if a shotgun microphone is used the result will generally also be poor audio. Don't forget that on a long lens your subject might look close, but without a sound operator holding a boom the shotgun microphone is still located on top of the smartphone, exactly where the operator is standing, possibly a long distance from the sound source.

Being close to the source is not always enough to record clean audio, especially if your subject is moving about in a developing scene. You'll need to ensure that you can move with the subject and that s/he is facing the microphone when they speak. If you can't do either of those two things you might need a different solution, maybe a radio microphone. Hence, it's important to survey the recording location and make a quick assessment of sound requirements and any impediments to recording clean audible sound. Because mojos work with breaking stories a location recce is not always possible. So a survey might simply mean keeping one eye open from the moment you set foot on location.

Now for the first rule of location sound recording: aim to record in a location without too much superfluous or ambient noise. In a drama the director might ask for more than one take on the dialogue to get the inflection right and then have it post-synced. But recording location sound is often a one-time only opportunity to cover evolving actuality, so mojos need to be prepared.

In short, the key to recording great audio is to know the answers to the following questions:

- **Are you a one-person operator or will you have a sound recordist? As a one-person band your audio-recording options are limited and you will be very busy.**
- **Will your camera microphone be OK, or do you need extra microphones, like lavalieres, to record clean sound?**
- **What's the location? A noisy road, quiet but remote jungle, rock band, maybe a football match or an isolated desert lacking back-up facilities?**

Once you understand the recording parameters you will be able to devise an audio-recording strategy.

Ivo's Tip: The quicker you decide about your sound parameters the more time you'll have to think about other elements.

RECORDING STRATEGY FOR AN INTERVIEW

Often news crews and documentary makers have a second and third person on the crew – reporter (producer), camera and sound. Some producer reporters record their own sound and only use a cameraperson. Video journalists can often do the lot – report, shoot and record sound. Mojos fall into the latter category. Basically, this means that if you hold the camera and ask questions, you won't be able to hold a boom pole. Hence, you'll need also to consider access. This will be your first hurdle. With access – the ability to get in close to film and interact – you can overcome many audio problems and won't need a boom. Without it you will need to consider not only how you will record the location audio, but whether you will be able to use it as your primary audio.

Any location sound problems a mojo might have are compounded when there is a need to record an interview. Conducting an interview will be dealt with in Chapter 8, but it will require a strategy, so I've listed a few quick tips for recording interview audio.

Recording an interview is the stock and trade of any journalist. A sit-down or walking interview is always a challenge because we often spend too long setting it up – deciding on the shot and the lighting – and we run out of time to think about the interview or the audio. The key to getting good interview audio is summarized below:

- *Knowing your subject*: **helps put them and you at ease and will help you get relevant information.**

131

- *Correct microphones*: ensure that your audio will be on mic and free of background noise (see later in this chapter).
- *Recording in a quite place*: helps with audio quality, relaxes your subject and helps the journalist concentrate on the interview.
- *Recording lots of B roll*: is the key to the interview and will help you edit unwanted audio glitches or noises, extend or shorten the interview and create dynamic **UPSOTS.**
- *Access*: being in close to the subject creates less room for unwanted audio and also enables the journalist *to feel the interview.*
- *Atmos track*: helps create smooth audio edits – you should try to record between 30 and 60 seconds of the ambient or natural sound at every location. This track is used to lay underneath dialogue to create a seamless audio base between dialogue edits and different types of dialogue – **VO** and sync audio. This *atmos* track will help smooth the audio transitions.

Ivo's Tip: The basic rule of sound recording is to record somewhere relatively quiet. If you can't, place the microphone as close to the subject as possible, to eliminate any unwanted background noise.

AUDIO GEAR

If you watch your favorite scene from any film or TV show with the sound off, you soon discover that moving images without audio are not very emotionally stimulating. Sound is key to creating a dynamic and emotional scene, one where the audio information is clearly audible. To achieve this you will need to follow the few tips mentioned above, but you'll also need the right equipment.

Today's smartphones have excellent onboard omnidirectional microphones that record clean and present audio if they are used up close and if there is no extraneous noise. But on location where ambient noise is often a problem and where the distance from your subject may vary, a third-party cardioid (directional mic) will usually work best.

A number of fancy audio apps are available (we will discuss a few), but they have little bearing on the quality of the recorded sound, except possibly being able to switch on an attenuator (which many good-quality mics have). Where audio apps can be useful is at the post-production stage (see Chapter 10).

Ivo's Tip: Ultra-directional or super-cardioid mics are best for external locations, directional or cardioid mics for interior; and non-directional or omnidirectional mics for cramped interiors without too much ambient noise.

CHOOSING THE RIGHT MICROPHONE

As effective as on-board microphones are, always try to use a more professional plug-in microphone. The mic you choose will mostly depend on your job. As a mojo you will probably use your smartphone's in-built microphone more often than not. But, at the very least, you should carry a third-party shotgun microphone in your kit. This can be the small two-inch microphone that ships with the mCamLite (see Chapter 4).

While a sound recordist will suggest you need to pin a lavaliere or a radio mic onto your subject, the reality, even with professional news crews, is very different. Even though using an onboard mic (one mounted on the camera) is rarely as effective as pinning a lavaliere or radio mic onto your subject, sticking a shotgun mic onto your smartphone will improve audio recording considerably. It will also make mojo a much more mobile experience than when using a cabled lavaliere microphone.

Here are a number of microphone options and situations where they might be used.

Shotgun Microphones

Shotgun microphones have a cardioid or super-cardioid pattern, which means that they are directional and because of this they are generally found on video cameras and used by news crews, video and mobile journalists. The disadvantage of directional mics is that they tend to pick up echo in tight interior locations and they need to be focused on axis – pointed at the subject being recorded.

Figure 6.3 Shotgun microphone.

Courtesy Rode

There are many examples of shotgun microphones and I have included a few that most mojos can afford and that we have tested:

- **The VideoMic Pro by Rode is a versatile shotgun microphone that is about 6 inches long with a three-way level control that offers −10dB, 0dB, and +20dB modes. This enables the mic to be attenuated when recording loud music like live bands, or when used for low audio or DSLR cameras. It also has a two-step high pass filter to negate the impact of low-frequency hum, like camera motor noise. The microphone's only drawback is its plastic construction and rubber mounts, which tend to come away from the body. It plugs into the smartphone's headphone jack via a 3.5 mm plug, but you'll need a TRS to TRRS conversion cable. You will need a dead-cat if you want to use this or any shotgun microphone in windy conditions. The microphone will run for 70 hours on one 9v battery. Price US$220.**
- **The Sennheiser MKE400 is even smaller than the Rode and made of steel. Its small size makes it ideal for smartphone use. Like the Rode mic it comes with a horseshoe attachment with a ¼ thread. It has two sensitivity settings, runs for more than 300 hours on one AAA battery, weighs just 200 grams and will fit easily into a small camera bag. It also requires a TRRS cable. Price US$200.**
- **Cheaper versions: a number of smaller shotgun mics are available. These can range from the two-inch offering that comes with the mCAMLite (iPhone cradle) and costs about $35 if bought separately, to the Audio Technica AT99131S, a solid metal-bodied mic that costs about US$80. These microphones get their power from the smartphone and as long as you have smartphone power, they will work.**

Any of the above microphones will do the job if you are close to your subject. The first two include attenuation switches and will record much cleaner audio when recording live music. The difference between these two microphones really comes down to size and build-quality. The windscreen on the Rode is more effective, but in windy conditions both mics will benefit from the addition of a Windjammer, or DeadCat-type wind stopper.

Ivo's Tip: When using a shotgun it's important to point it at the audio source. For this reason beware of XY-type mics that plug into a smartphone and point away from the source. They are great when recording audio alone as they can be directed at source, or if used on a third-party recording device, which can be directed in the direction of the audio source.

Lavaliere Microphones

The first lavaliere microphones were cigar-like tubes. Today they are small inconspicuous omnidirectional mics that are recording some of the most famous voices on television and radio. Sometimes called lapel mics, lavaliere mics come wired or wireless (discussed next).

There are two types of lavaliere microphones:

- **proximity – more authoritative sound with minimal background interference**
- **transparent – a much more natural-sounding mic that is more forgiving when used with people who speak away from the mic. The problem with transparent mics is that they are much more sensitive to background noise.**

Figure 6.4 **Rode Smart Lav
+ lavaliere microphone.**

Courtesy Rode

Wired lavaliere mics are mostly used in sit-down interviews where the camera is not moved and where the sound-recording device needs to be concealed. They can often be perfect for situations where presenters are demonstrating and require both hands free.

The benefit of using lavaliere mics is that they are generally placed on the lapel only inches from the subject's mouth. This means they are shielded from extraneous noise from behind the subject. To provide a back-up, lavaliere mics can be used in conjunction with shotgun mics on devices offering multi-track audio recording.

Ivo's Tip: Lavaliere mics can be affected by the rustle of clothing, so if you don't have to hide the lavaliere under clothing, don't.

Lavaliere mics can be cardioid, but are mostly omnidirectional, so that when a journalist moves their head while speaking, there is no resulting dip in volume. Lavalieres can be made small enough to hide behind clothing, or stuck to skin or material with Stickies (Rycote). If you are hiding a lavaliere using Stickies, loop the cable to create some strain relief and stick that down to the clothing to stop the clothes rustle.

Ivo's Tip: Spread your thumb and small finger into the hang loose sign (about 8 inches) and place the tip of your thumb on your mouth. Where the tip of the pinky touches your shirt is where you pin the lavaliere.

I've tested four lavaliere mics at different price points:

- **Rode Smart Lav + is a very good lavaliere microphone made for the iPhone. It has a crisp sound and for US$60 represents excellent value.**
- **Azden EX-503i Studio Pro Lapel Mic is another almost studio quality mic made especially with a smartphone TRRS connector. At US$50 it is an excellent alternative**
- **Rode lavaliere is the most expensive and professional version that Rode makes. This microphone has a very natural sound and a number of capsules can be fitted to enable use with varying devices. You may need a TRRS adapter. At US$280 this is a mid-price point and an excellent option.**
- **Sanken CS011D is one of the best lavaliere microphones I have used. It has a bright and present sound. Sometimes I feel it is a little more sibilant than the other microphones. Price US$380.**

An excellent resource describing the different sound quality of four popular lavaliere microphones can be found at this link: www.youtube.com/watch?v=1djyJxV3hV4. You may need converter cables which can be found here: www.kvconnection.com.

Ivo's Tip: If you can't get a lavaliere microphone and can't get your camera in close enough put your shotgun microphone on a Rode or Manfrotto mini mic stand and place that just out of frame (you may need an extension cable).

Radio Microphones

Radio microphones are the most versatile of all lavaliere microphones because the addition of a transmitter and a receiver enables journalists to move about without being tied to the camera. It's the same freedom that occurred in the 1960s when pioneer documentary maker and news cameraman D.A. Pennebaker untethered his sound recordist from his 16 mm camera to enable both to move independently.

Figure 6.5 **Testing the Sony UWPD11 Radio Microphones for mojo work using a smartphone and mCAMLite.**

Ivo Burum

Radio mics can take a bit of time to set up but once set you can walk away and get on with the job. They can suffer from frequency

139

issues, especially when used in high RF areas, like busy cities or war zones. But generally if you buy a reputable brand you'll find a useable frequency.

There are many price points and brands of radio microphones. We will discuss one entry-level set and two mid-range more professional versions.

The first point I would make is that you should buy a digital radio microphone if you can afford one. Second, I don't think you need to spend more than US$600–750 to get a good radio microphone set. Finally, you can always upgrade the actual microphone and or capsule at a later stage.

One aspect of wireless sound recording is that you may have to calibrate the sensitivity to get super clean sound into the camera. This exact setting will differ camera to camera, but the principle remains the same.

Ivo's Tip: If you are using a DSLR turn your microphone transmitter down to about –10db and your receiver to about –4db. Then go to the manual audio setting of the DSLR and dial the setting to zero and then two clicks up. The aim is to reduce the amount of work the DSLR pre amp needs to do. You will need to test this system with each DSLR of smartphone as they will all differ on the level of attenuation required.

I have grouped radio mics into two categories, entry level and professional mid-range:

Cheaper:

- **Azden WM Pro only has two frequencies and this may pose problems in high RF locations. The sound is flat and lifeless with little presence. This is an entry-level radio microphone with out a VU meter and costs US$149, but still does the job albeit with a great deal of background noise.**
- **Azden WR32-Pro is a dual-frequency, dual-channel radio microphone system. It enables journalist and subject to be on radio mic with both signals travelling back to one receiver. It also enables one of the body packs to be replaced by the WM/T-Pro handheld transmitter. You'll need to split the signal for cameras with two-track recording otherwise both mic signals will be recorded on one track, Price is US$340 plus the hand-held mic and transmitter.**

More expensive:

- **Sennheiser EW112PG3B has over 1600 frequencies to choose from. It is a system that is often used as a back-up by professional sound recordists. The body has a rugged metal housing and the system can be extended to include hand held or wireless hand-held options. I found that at distance or when moving out of line of sight this system can begin to break up. Otherwise it offers clean sound. Price US$630.**
- **Sony UWPD11 incorporates digital audio processing and is the latest UWP line from Sony. I have been using the analog version for 20 years without issues in very high RF areas. The UWP-D11 has a very wide tuning range (widest in its class), and has a much easier user interface than its predecessor. It has colored LED**

distortion indicators, USB charging and a much more rugged feel than the G3. In our test the UWP-D11 was much clearer, without any static for a much further distance than the G3. The receiver has a very clear monitor output that is identical to what's being recorded on camera. It comes with a decent microphone, which can be upgraded. The UWP-D11 is a diversity system that uses two antennas to achieve stable reception. The sound recording from this system is sweeter than the Sennheiser. The complete UWP-D system includes a wireless hand-mic and a plug-on transmitter with an XLR connection to any suitable microphone such as a regular hand-mic or shotgun microphone. The transmitter can operate for eight hours and the receiver for six hours on 2AA batteries. The UWP-D11 is priced at approximately US$600.

Ivo's Tip: Generally speaking the above systems require a method to affix the microphone to the camera. On a DSLR this will be via a horseshoe mount and for an iPhone you'll need a housing Phocus, mCamLite, the versatile Shoulderpod S1 or Rode Grip Pro (all four discussed in Chapter 4).

Studio Microphones

From a mojo point of view studio mics will often sit on a desktop in an edit suite, or in a voice-over booth. In the context of producing mojo stories, more often than not studio-type microphones will be used to record narration. As most mojo stories will be produced and delivered from the field, most mojos will not use these mics, except when developing their UGS into something longer, or combining it with other stories into a user-generated program (UGP), produced back at the office.

The Apogee MiC and the Rode NT USB are the only two I have used with the iPhone and can recommend. Both are studio-quality cardioid microphones (semi-directional) for iDevices designed for vocal and acoustic instrument recording, the Apogee with a PureDIGITAL connection. The two microphones vary greatly in size so if this is an option, and it may be for a mojo, the Apogee will be for you. I use the Rode NT USB in the edit suite. A microphone comparison video is available at this link: www.focalpress.com/cw/burum. Listen to sample audio at this link: http://smartmojo.com/2015/02/13/microphone-comparo-101/

Figure 6.6 Size comparison between the Rode NT USB and the Apogee MiC.

Ivo Burum

Ivo's Tip: Leave the pop shield on to avoid popping and Rode's bass-type hum. Best used in a controlled studio-type environment.

DUAL RECORDING

The above options are based on recording audio directly onto the iPhone's hard disk or a DSLR camera's SD card. A couple of other options using digital recorders and or USB mixers to record dual audio are worth discussing:

1. Digital audio recorder: Many portable digital audio recorders are on the market and range in price from under $100 to more than $600. These can be used to record extra or back-up sound. The two we'll discuss here are the Zoom H1 and the Rode XY microphone.

   • Zoom H1: This is a plastic device that feels as if it will break apart if it's dropped. But the audio quality is superb and remarkable for something that sells for around US$120. The H1 can record linear PCM (WAV) files at up to 96kHz (the H5 will record four tracks of audio). With its directional pattern, it is an excellent alternative recorder for a smartphone or DSLR. Providing up to ten hours of record time from a single AA battery, it is ideal for location recording. With the benefit of simultaneous onboard back-up recording, its diverse pre-amp settings enable far greater control over audio recording than that offered by either a smartphone or DSLR. It has the added advantage of being able to be disconnected from the camera and placed close to a sound source, while the camera roves for coverage. Later the file is transferred using AirStash (see Chapter 4) and married to video during the edit or used as non-sync audio.

- **Rode XY: If the iPhone is used as a recording device for another smartphone or DSLR, a Rode XY microphone, which can be directed towards the sound source, is an excellent digital microphone choice. At US$140 this would also be a great video mic option if it could pivot 90 degrees off the iPhone toward the action. As it is, it's a much better mic for recording high-quality music or lectures, unless used as a second microphone pointed at the sound source.**

2. Mixer: Another form of dual recording is achieved using a mixer like the Roland Duo Capture EX ($200AUD). It will capture two independent tracks of audio. This would require a two-lapel microphone set-up and would be an ideal choice for a formal interview set up in a controlled environment.

Figure 6.7 Roland Duo Capture EX two-track mixer interface next to a smartphone to show its compact size.

Ivo Burum

Finally, recording clean location audio involves treating sound as a key element and not an afterthought. This attitude and praxis begins long before arriving at location. On location it's all about listening, having the right equipment and being close to the sound source, so you can hear and relate to the story.

Here are my favorite tips for sound recording:

- **Choose the right microphone.**
- **Don't settle for the camera's microphone.**
- **Place the microphone as close as possible to the sound source and keep checking its axis to the source.**
- **If you are using lavaliere mics be careful to avoid the rustle of clothing.**
- **If using a shotgun mic get the main dialogue in an MCU because that will mean you will be close enough.**
- **Do a technical check before you begin every interview.**
- **Where possible use both shotgun and lavaliere mics.**
- **If you have time and need to, record a second take.**
- **If possible always listen via headphones during the recording.**
- **Check the recording immediately after every interview and before you wrap location.**
- **Record a buzz track at every location that's at least 30 seconds long to help make the audio cuts seamless.**
- **Stagger your audio edits (see Chapter 10).**

Because recording narration involves writing to pictures it is dealt with in more detail in Chapters 7, 9 and 10; but here is a summary of key tips you may want to consider:

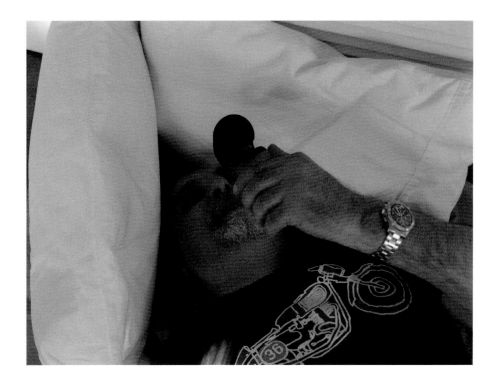

Figure 6.8 Ivo recording
audio using pillows to
baffle echo and sound.

Ivo Burum

- Narration is always best recorded in an audio booth, or at a quiet location without echo where the sound is dampened. You may have a room that is too live in which case you can put a towel or a blanket over your head, or record between two large pillows, or two mattresses shaped in a V. Or you can do what I used to do on *Foreign Correspondent or Gardening Australia*, and record narration on location, in a quiet field or an alley (this method will work well as long as you record a buzz track).
- Make the script simple without too many alliterations.
- Make sure the script is conversational.
- Stand up while recording and use your hands if that helps.
- Have a drink on standby to alleviate sticky tongue.
- Relax and slow down.

- **Mark all takes and definitely mark the best to save time in edit.**
- **Pop can be eliminated by moving the mic slightly off center.**
- **Roll into retake immediately after a fluff.**
- **Breathe out before a take.**
- **If you cannot remember your lines, take your mind off the read. One way is to pinch yourself hard off camera while you are doing the take. If standing, put a stone in your shoe so you feel the pain during the read.**

In conclusion, the more thought you give to sound the better your pictures will look. The audience will forgive bad pictures if your subject is compelling; what they will never accept is poor sound. And the subject is always more compelling when they can be heard clearly. Two decades ago we needed a lot of expensive gear and a sound recordist to get good sound. Today recording sound can be done much cheaper, but it should never be seen as less important than pictures. Knowing what equipment to use and how to record audio correctly is still the key to getting good location sound.

Remember, if you record bad sound you can't really fix it. Aim to record the best possible location sound. Try to avoid extraneous ambient sound and fix any sound issues on location, not in post-production. Use the right microphone placed as close as possible to the sound source. Make sure that if you are using unbalanced mics your cables should not exceed three meters in length. If you use a double system – that is a separate recording device like a Zoom attached to the smartphone or sitting near the source – be mindful about how you will combine audio and pictures in the edit.

I conclude this chapter by stressing the importance of preparation, and nowhere is this more important than at the story development phase, which is the subject of the next chapter.

REFERENCE

AFTRS. 2014. "Introduction to Location Sound Recording." AFTRS.

CHAPTER 7

SCRAP

THE ELEMENTS IN MOJO STORYTELLING

Ivo Burum

SUMMARY

This chapter introduces and develops the basic building blocks of mojo storytelling, and shows how to develop multimedia stories in a multi-planar form. This requires a basic story development philosophy like SCRAP, which stands for Story, Character, Resolution, Actuality and Production. It also requires an understanding of how to use basic multimedia story elements: actuality, interviews, B roll, piece to camera (PTC) and narration. Understanding these aspects of multimedia storytelling will enable mojos to develop, identify and create powerful user-generated stories (UGS), which is explored next in this chapter.

WHAT ARE MOJO STORIES?

Author Robert McKee says, "Story isn't a flight from reality but a vehicle that carries us on our search for reality, our best effort to make sense out of anarchy of existence" (1999: 12). Mojo stories, which can be made by almost anyone, do exactly that; they help us make sense of the reality about us. In a way understanding mojo skills helps us to better utilize the potential of the millions of hours of user-generated content (UGC) that's zapping across virtual network societies: in essence to create sense of digital online anarchy.

Telling mojo stories is very different from writing print stories, yet both use some common skills. Some journalism lecturers and teachers of storytelling will tell you that the big difference is that digital stories don't use the inverted pyramid (a journalistic style where facts are presented in descending order of importance). They suggest you don't have to inform the reader about *who, what, where, when and why* in the opening paragraph, as usually happens in print journalism. This is not necessarily true. I've made thousands of short video and digital stories and still like to set them up as quickly as possible. The Five Ws and One H (who, what, where, when, why and how) simply tell the audience what you are going to tell them during the story, almost like an intro at the head of a television program, which briefly describes what's on in that program. It's a summary of the key elements and is often the news or what's most topical.

Here is an example from *Missing Persons Unit*, an investigative police series, on which I was the executive producer.

Table 7.1 Program introduction describing the quick information flow.

Vision	Audio
Titles tease	Nar: Tonight on *Missing Persons Unit* . . .
A mother makes her missing child's bed and picks up a picture of an 8-year old girl.	In Perth, a 13-year-old's mum is beside herself
CU mum.	Mum sync: (crying) Katie's dead I know she's dead
An old man stands at the front gate staring down the street	Nar: In Adelaide a loving grandmother with dementia vanishes.
CU pic of old lady MCU husband distraught	Husband sync: If you see her please be gentle . . . Martha I love you.
Cops digging in a park	Nar: And in Sydney a gruesome end to a 20-year mystery
WS grave CU cop looking down	Cop sync: Yes I think we've finally found Cheryl.
Titles breaker graphics "1 person is reported missing every 18 minutes . . ."	Music: sting and play out.

I wrote every program of *Missing Persons Unit*, which was a number one series on Australian television, and while every program felt the same, each was nuanced differently. The story elements found in the above introduction, which are common to most introductions, are a basic news lead and a scene setter. This information works because it is laced with a startling statement made by someone affected by the story, supported by graphic – it must be real – footage.

The big difference between print and video is that multimedia or UGS are multi-planar and can be laced with many elements such as audio, video, interviews, actuality and graphics, working together on many planes of content (video, audio, music, graphics). Print stories are generally constructed so that the further you read the less relevant the information becomes. In multimedia storytelling, even when working in a non-linear timeline, you can't chop away from the bottom of the story as easily as you can with print. The multimedia elements are more visceral and their position in the story timeline is relative across a number of planes. Notwithstanding this, multimedia stories still rely on a style that sets them up quickly, makes them dynamic, and assists fast turn-around.

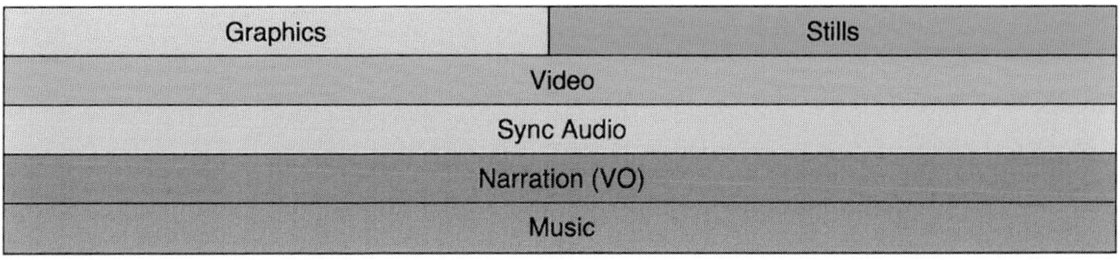

Graphics	Stills
Video	
Sync Audio	
Narration (VO)	
Music	

Figure 7.1 **Multimedia storytelling is multi-planar.**

Ivo Burum

While many print journalists are great at telling stories, they are not as efficient at recognizing the different multimedia elements that make up a UGS. They don't immediately have the complete set of skills required to tell mojo stories (see Table 7.2). Nor are they immediately comfortable with the workflow used to develop mojo-type stories. I often hear journalists say, "But I've already interviewed the person on the phone." When I ask, "What about the pictures?" the usual response is a moment's silence. This chapter will introduce you to the basic steps used to create mojo UGS.

Table 7.2 Competencies

1. Research	4. Record Audio
2. Write	5. Edit
3. Record Vision	6. Publish

VOYEUR AS STORYTELLER

How much of today's mobile UGC creation is the result of the popularity of reality TV – a type of program about supposed real life – and what might happen to you or me in a staged circumstance or event? *Candid Camera* (1948) was a Cold War format that recorded ordinary people in extraordinary and staged circumstances that functioned to tell people to stop worrying about being watched.

Reality TV is arguably doing the same. The "it could be me" aspect of reality TV has been a great part of its appeal. This fascination with projecting private images in the public sphere is also partly responsible for the high volume of UGC that citizens are uploading to the Internet. Because viewers see an element of their own lives in reality shows, what unites this range of programming is primarily its discursive, visual and technological claim to "the real." A range of "it could be me" moments in what is essentially a contrived, event-driven commercial space. This manifestation of self-marketing, learned from reality TV shows, may be an element that makes mobile uploads popular and fuels this highly contested and largely self-obsessed online space.

My own history as a program maker and storyteller mirrors the stylistic and technological development of factual television. In the early 1990s I was a pioneer of formatted self-shot television in Australia with series like *Home Truths*, *Nurses*, *Race Around Oz* and later *After the Fires* (all for ABC TV). These series, which taught ordinary citizens (consumers) to create content for broadcast (become producers), were precursors to current UGC forms, albeit destined for free-to-air television and not the web.

Jeff Lowrey, a participant in *Home Truths*, one of Australia's first forays into formatted self-shot television, says, "It gave a working-class bloke like me without any experience in TV an opportunity to tell my own story from a very different perspective" (in Burum 1994). Jeff may have been an early victim of the digital sublime, but 2.5 billion smartphone users who uploaded tens of million hours of video in 2014 share his view.

From 1995 when the Internet became a public tool for communication it became a lot easier for ordinary people to tell stories. People could finally bypass network gatekeepers and publish their own UGC online. Today's UGC producers, those who New York University journalism professor Jay Rosen says are no longer the audience, are not waiting to be asked to appear on TV shows. They are turning their cameras on themselves, creating their own candid camera moments, which are destined for YouTube and other social media.

The availability of this relatively free and limitless platform has increased experimentation in UGC production even further. As technology got smaller and more powerful, smartphones were able to record, edit and publish, high-quality video and audio more cheaply and immediately. A new group of citizen storytellers found the technology addictive and the lure of ready-made publishing platforms, like YouTube, irresistible.

In theory these opportunities created the potential for a more democratic and diverse publishing model, in a more robust *market place of ideas.* Professor Philip Napoli, head of journalism at Rutgers University, said the assumption was that an audience with diverse content production options consumes a diversity of content, which promotes attention and exposure to a diversity of views.

Media critic Robert McChesney believes these assumptions are *central to democratic theory and practice*. New technologies, he says, are becoming society's *central nervous system* in ways previously unimaginable. It is a time where old communication institutions are collapsing and where, for the next coupe of decades, great change is possible.

And herein lies the conundrum. With every possible *upside*, there is often a *downside*. The flexibility that digital technology provides – in this case communications technology – can also have a negative impact on the craft of storytelling. As renowned filmmaker Ken Burns observes, "We love the new technology and the accessibility to everybody – the democratization of the process. But at the same time, we see, particularly with regard to the Internet and video, the way in which the technological tail is now beginning to wag the dog. I think we've lost touch with story" (cited in Stubbs 2002: 89).

Storytelling expert Robert McKee adds, "While the ever-expanding reach of the media now gives us the opportunity to send stories beyond borders and languages to hundreds of millions, the overall quality of story-telling is being eroded" (1999: 13). This technological drowning of craft partly results from cheap digital technology that enables almost anyone to pick up a mobile and publish online kludge like gossip.

McKee notes Aristotle's observation, more than two thousand years ago, that when storytelling goes bad the result is decadence. While not all UGC is kludge, or gossip, to a large extent what exists up there is, what Stuart Gant calls, online chaos. Hence there is a need to more fully understand the potential of using mojo skills and smartphones to tell more relevant, more diverse stories. That's the intention of this chapter, to help transform online decadence into powerful UGS.

SCRAP: HOW TO DEVELOP STRONG NEWS LIKE UGS

The most common mistake many video storytellers make is that they often lose sight of their story by producing it for too many audiences. In doing so they risk suffocating creative energy and even killing the story focus. With the millions of hours of gossip like UGC on the Internet, it seems that story has made way for unfocused fragmented citizen witness moments.

Whether your idea is about a character, or an event, your first step is to understand the story, who will tell it and whom it is about. In my experience, more often than not, stories begin at home with the age-old phrase "I know a person who." But we quickly realize that even if our short UGS is a profile, we need to focus on one specific moment or aspect about the person and build our more complete story around that. To help us in this search and to make sure that our story is achievable I use a tool that I call SCRAP (Story, Character, Resolution, Actuality and Production).

On the road and shooting on the run, we need an easy to use checklist like SCRAP, which is a first step to focusing story. If you don't get that right your story will most likely end up on the scrap heap. Table 7.3 describes the SCRAP matrix and how this relates to the story's Five Ws.

As described in the table, if we look at SCRAP more carefully and more as a set of research questions, we see that it provides answers to our Five Ws:

> *Story* describes the *what* element: *what's happening and what's the story.*
> *Character* tells us *who is in the story* and this helps inform the story elements.
> *Resolution* describes the structure and the *why and how* aspects of the story.

Actuality is the content we film and gather to tell the story and provides the *who, what, where, when and why* of our story.

Production can describe *how, where and when* you tell the story.

Table 7.3 SCRAP: a road map for UGS.

	Five Ws	Description
Story	What's the story?	A clear focus about the purpose of the story is needed so that we can identify and form the character(s).
Characters	Who are they?	Often this is the starting point of your story, *I know someone who*, or *Have you heard about?* This requires the storyteller go back to the *story* step, to find focus, characters, places and events. Knowing the characters informs the story and its logistics.
Resolution	Knowing the beginning, middle and end is knowing *why*.	If your story is current it will evolve and take shape as you cover it, so, how can you know how it will resolve? You can't know that completely. Let's say, hypothetically, we are producing a story on Valentino Rossi's love of go-kart racing and specifically about his first competition. We might begin by having his many go-karts loaded into a semi-trailer, his cook preparing his breakfast and a packed lunch. We know there will be training, the heats and the final. We know the day will end with awards. What we don't know is whether it will be a fair race, or whether Rossi will end up on the podium, or in the hospital. So we can research a structure, which provides the form and the scope, to plan the day, but which enables the flexibility for *actuality* and for *story* to develop at its own pace.
Actuality	Where, what, when and who will I film?	Actuality is the live evolving action that happens at the scene, which you can't set up. It can include some B Roll (overlay) and on-the-scene interviews. It is key to creating story dynamics and currency.
Production	How will I make the story?	Knowing how the story might play out, who the characters are, what needs to be filmed and when and where is critical to being able to meet deadlines.

Ivo's Tip: If you stop thinking about the Five Ws and One H as being part of the inverted pyramid story structure and more as a research formula, it becomes a valuable tool for multimedia storytelling.

THE IMPORTANCE OF THE 5WS AS RESEARCH

Answering the Five Ws is something all storytellers do; it's just that journalists do it in one paragraph (often the first) and generally more quickly than many other writers or producers, except maybe people producing ads. But as Robert McKee writes in his book, *Story*, all writers, no matter what field they work in, need to understand the *who, what, when, where and why* of their story.

Let's look at this lead and example of the Five Ws and One H of a story:

> A 27-year-old Croatian panel beater was arrested at Sydney Airport last night in possession of a large bag of diamonds hidden in a false pocket of his suit jacket.

Who: a 27-year-old panel beater. Even if a story is about an event it is often best told through the eyes of a person, so knowing *who* the person(s) is (are) gives it a human angle more people can relate to. In a longer piece we provide even more information about *who* our character is.

Possibly, in the above example, the man turns out to be an Interpol agent working undercover; maybe he is a drug courier, maybe the diamonds were planted. Our longer story would explain and identify *who* the other players are – *who's* involved and *who's* affected. A mojo might also consider *who* the best people are to tell the story. In the above example the *who* could include: the Croatian panel beater, the arresting police man, maybe a witness, family in Australia, a local diamond expert, a customs worker.

┃ Who would you interview in the diamond story?

What: he was arrested for possession of concealed diamonds. The "what" element goes to the heart of journalism and news: *what* is worth reporting, or watching?

┃ Would the story have got a run if the man had been arrested with salami in his pocket?

Ivo's Tip: No matter "what" has happened, it's only ever going to be half as interesting as it should be if your "who" is boring or if your "where" is not local.

Where: Sydney Airport – the closer a story is to home the more important it is. The above story would not be as interesting to Americans, or in Australia if the panel beater was arrested in, let's say, Zagreb.

Ivo's Tip: UGS are videos so we rely on pictures, or visual proof, to show and tell us where we are.

When: last night – gives the story a place in time; in this case it gives the story currency. If you're a mojo working for one of the 24-hour news channels, or for a social media platform, you'll be trying to report or tweet the news first. So identifying currency is very important. For example, on a television series called *Missing*

Persons Unit (Nine Network, Australia), we used to remind our audience of the *when* by telling them that "One person is reported missing every 18 minutes." For example: "Of the 80 people reported missing each day [*when*], six of them will be teenagers, just like Rachel [*who*] . . ." Using *when* in this context adds currency and increases the stakes.

Why: helps explain what's happening. In our Sydney Airport example, we might also find out *why* the panel beater had the diamonds. Maybe they were planted on him (in a hidden pocket). The *why* is often the most fascinating element and helps a story stand out from a similar story produced by another reporter.

How: explains the sequence of events. In our example, we might reveal that our panel beater looked nervous and became jittery. Maybe he wet his pants. We might find out *how* and even *why*

Figure 7.2 **The Five Ws.**

Ivo Burum

161

he was arrested; maybe police were tipped off. We might eventually find out *how* he came to have the diamonds. Finally, planning *how* your story information is revealed is essential when producing multi-planar, multimedia stories.

THE FIVE-POINT PLAN

Before you begin collating story elements it's helpful to create a simple five-point structural plan. This plan includes an introduction, a story development point, a middle section, another story development point and an end. It works like a tree trunk to hold the story structure together. You will find this especially helpful when out on that branch of creativity collecting inspirational media and wondering what you will you do with all your new content. Your story spine will help determine whether the new media is relevant and if so how to use it. It may mean adjusting the spine, your plan and your perspective. You may need to look at the relationship between the three faces of mojo story construction: SCRAP, the Five Ws and the Five-Point Plan.

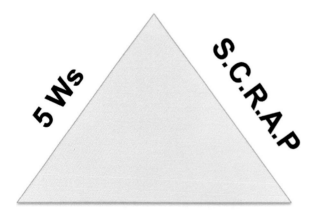

Figure 7.3 Mojo story triangle.

Ivo Burum

Knowing the three faces of the story triangle will help define your focus. Which story we decide to make will impact on the information (elements) we choose to record. As columnist Tim Harrower explains (2010), the same story told by different interviewees can have a completely different focus and outcome. For example, we can tell a number of stories about a group of university graduates: a story about job prospects (politics and economics); one about the ceremony (fashion); or the parties that follow (entertainment); or we could simply follow graduates and their families (profiles). We can also marry our interviewees to produce a longer story featuring their collective experiences.

Choose a theme and see how many different story angles you can come up with. Each angle may require different characters, specific to the story angle.

BASIC STORY ELEMENTS

After developing a story focus the next step is to gather the elements that will be used to create the story and a signature story bounce – the stylistic rhythm that's usually agreed when a format is set. This meter, beat, or what I call *story bounce*, is a timing thing that occurs as a result of the placement and duration of *story elements* on the timeline. The story bounce is a series of unfolding sequences (of information and emotion) each with their own rhythm, designed to affect the viewer at a given point of the story. How elements are used (overlay, actuality, interview, narration, PTC) and when (the order of delivery between story elements and structure) will determine *story bounce*.

Ivo's Tip: You should think about the story bounce when covering the story – what does the audience need to know next and how is this best conveyed – on location.

Following is a list of basic story elements that can be used in any multimedia story to create story bounce. The degree to which you focus on one element more than another will impact the style of your story.

Stand-Up or Piece to Camera (PTC)

The PTC is shot at location and is often used to:

- **provide information where no other vision exists;**
- **set the reporter in a location;**
- **compress or expand a level of information;**
- **highlight or introduce a character or make a point.**

PTCs are generally seen at the head or the end of a news story, but can occur at any stage. They should appear where they fit best and where they are needed most. For example, in a current affairs story I produced in Sicily, about the Mafia, we used a PTC outside a house to describe how a young boy who had been imprisoned in the house might have suffered during his two years in captivity. We used the PTC because there was no other footage and because we needed to convey the emotional weight of this tragedy. We used the weight of the reporter's words to create emotion. The walk and talk style of the PTC showed how local people must have walked by the house and the captive boy, time and again, without noticing.

A few basic rules apply when recording a PTC:

- *Background*: **Don't do your PTC in front of some nondescript backdrop that requires the audience to guess where you are, because the audience needs all the help it can get, especially in a short news story. Shoot the PTC in a way that shows story-specific action in the background of the shot: make the shot a little wider, or pan into it from frame left or right, or settle into your final position to one side of frame, leaving story-related background action visible.**
- *Dead air*: **Be careful that you don't have** *dead air* **around your PTC in the edit – no empty pause before you begin or after you finish. Overlap the outgoing and the incoming vision slightly in the edit to avoid dead air. Use audio to help transitions and help fill potential dead spots.**
- *Tracking PTC*: **Experiment with walking and talking PTCs – don't make them all static. Even a couple of steps will make the shot more dynamic. Learn to do this working on your own.**
- *Script*: **Learn your words and don't look at a script while reading a PTC. If you do need to look at notes, make it obvious (on camera) that it's part of the PTC. If you can't remember your words think of something else and the words will come. If you write the PTC on location, pick three or four key words for the PTC. Thinking about the story rather than the words generally helps. If that doesn't work and if you are walking and talking put a stone in your shoe, so that you can feel it when you walk, and the words will come.**

Ivo's Tip: Practice PTCs in your car. As you pull up at a set of lights look around and make up a quick PTC about what's going on and what you see. Deliver it before the lights turn green.

Interviews

An interview provides immediacy, gravitas, expertise and/or a personal opinion. Who you decide to interview will affect the story balance. Some reporters call interviewees "sources" who give you a *grab* and you think you've *got the story*. Treat interviewees as storytellers and you'll inherently want to know more about them. Interviewees will respond better, give you relevant unexpected information and you'll want to set them up in location and shoot relevant B roll that describes their story. How we record interviews will be discussed at length in Chapter 8.

Ivo's Tip: Try using an interview a number of times across a story by asking the interviewee a question for the beginning, middle and end of your story. Write in and out of the best bits and cover the cuts with B roll about what the interviewees are saying.

Actuality

This is the video content that you don't need to set up. At an accident scene it could be paramedics, police and other services doing their job. It could be family at the scene and hysterical onlookers. Actuality gives the story currency and the dynamics it needs to hold an audience. It also shows the journalist on the

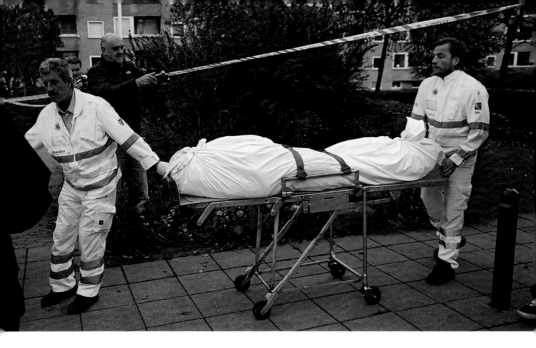

Figure 7.4 Ivo working as a mojo at a murder scene for *Ekstra Bladet* in Denmark.

Claus Bonnerup

scene as the news is happening. You can't ask the fire officer to put the fire out again because you are late on the scene. You need to be ready to record actuality immediately when you arrive. In the scene above I am shooting a story on an iPhone at the scene of a murder. Minutes later the network news camera man arrived late and while he set up his gear we edited and uploaded the story using the iPhone.

Ivo's Tip: Survey the scene and record the actuality that's most time-critical first. You will need to keep an eye open to make sure your interviewees don't disappear.

Overlay (B roll)

You can never have too much B roll, because with narration it is a key that enables the journalist to compress and expand story points. It's often said that B roll doesn't include footage of interviewees or on-camera talent. That's not always true as interviewees do appear in B roll. If the interviewee is talking about a football game and the score, or a fight on the field, your B roll might include

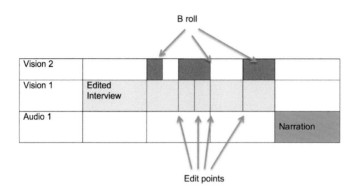

Figure 7.5 **Example of how to use B roll over edited interview.**

Ivo Burum

these aspects of the game and include the interviewee. B-roll shots that relate to aspects mentioned in the interview enable the journalist to show those points at various stages of the edit, to provide color and compression.

B roll is crucial for covering edits that we call jump cuts, which can occur in an interview that has been shortened. It is also used to cover content for legal reasons, or to highlight a point to create specific story bounce. Edits made in an interview can also be covered with a shot of the reporter listening, often referred to as a "noddy," but effectively this is also a form of B roll. A how to use B roll video is available at this link: www.focalpress.com/cw/burum.

Narration

BBC correspondent Alan Little says that all writing begins with making sure that you have something to say, and saying it with the right words. In video production you also need to use the right inflection and tone, making sure the structure, in particular the narration script is clear and simple. Writing for the web means that your story needs to be told in the first few paragraphs so that it works across platforms. This will impact the length of your sync grabs and your narration will be short and dynamic.

The writer begins by knowing what they want to say. Next is knowing what media you have to work with. Finally you need to be clear about story moments and bounce. Are you conveying emotion, drama, information and what's the genre? Your narration script will be key to hitting video sync triggers that set off an emotional, or dramatic story moment.

Narration is particularly important in a short piece where it is used to move the story quickly from one structural point to another. A glue that binds story elements, narration script helps create and maintain the story meter, or bounce, and is used to compress verbose interviews by linking choice grabs. You may hear the term "writing in and out of pictures." This refers to the process of linking narration to sync and is one of the journalist's strongest tools.

When writing a text story we write script and leave gaps for quotes. Writing for video is not unlike this. We write into pictures or choose sync voice grabs that are also like quotes. Just like in a written script, video narration links the major story elements, and drives the narrative. A good narration script highlights major story milestones. An early draft script will include the actual sync words, if the journalist has listened to these, or just the word "sync," which is between the narration grabs.

Because mojo is a picture medium a narration script does not need to state the obvious. Certainly avoid making the last words out of the narration the same as the first words of the sync (see Chapter 9). Even though your narration will be covered by B roll that relates to the narration, your sync grabs will help the story come alive. The description will generally happen in the sync.

Here is an example:

> Narration: "The bomb exploded as the patrol appeared (in the town square)."

Question: Do you have to tell the viewer the patrol entered the square and that it's an army patrol? Answer: Not if you can see this in B roll.

Question: We cut to sync from a witness — is it best to interview them in a quiet studio or at the window on the third floor of an apartment overlooking the square from where they watched the explosion? Answer: On location at the third floor window is best.

Sync: "I saw six of the soldiers die. Some were killed by the bomb, others were shot. One fell, then another and finally they were all down, bleeding, cut down, not moving. I was paralyzed with fear and couldn't move."

In this case the narration script for a video story, unlike for a radio story, is basically an introduction covered with story-specific B roll that leads to exciting sync. Your narration B roll (cover shots) doesn't always need to be silent. Narration script can be written in such a way to allow for a "sound-up."

For example: Let's say we have some news B roll of the soldiers being blown up and shot. We could break our narration as follows: "I saw six of the soldiers die" . . . insert vision and sound-up of explosion for about 3–4 seconds, then reintroduce sync . . . "some died from the bomb and others were shot" . . . insert vision with sound-up of shooting . . . then back to narration or sync.

Ivo's Tip: Always shoot your B roll with sound.

Narration script should be written in "active" voice. A "voice" is the form a verb takes and it can be "passive" or "active." It indicates whether the subject "performs" or "receives" action. An example of active voice is "The rebels shot the soldiers." The rebels (subject)

Table 7.4 How the above sequence might look like this in script form

Vision	Audio
B roll of a patrol of soldiers entering the square	Nar: I saw six of the soldiers die . . .
Same B roll . . . the bomb explodes and soldiers begin to fall (3 secs) we see soldiers screaming.	Natsot: (bomb explodes). A soldier cries out, "Over there!"
B roll wide soldiers being shot . . .	Nar: . . . some killed by the bomb, others by sniper fire
B roll of soldiers falling and yelling out to each other	Natsot: (shots fire and soldiers yelling) (cont.)

did the shooting (verb) is active. An example of passive voice is: "The soldiers were shot by the rebels." The soldiers (subject) were being shot (verb) is passive.

The reason for using active voice is that it's neater, less clumsy and it propels the reader into the story much quicker. Passive voice can be used when you don't want to, or can't, reveal the performer of an action, or when you want to emphasize the receiver. Finally, a passive voice will almost always consist of a form of the verb "to be." For example: active: "The rebel shot the soldier"; passive: "The soldier was shot by the rebel."

Narration is not the only element of a video script. In fact we have included many in this chapter that are used to paint, or write, the visual script. But narration is certainly the most useful of the tools a writer uses to integrate all the other elements into the script. Because narration is used to help create the structure or meter of a UGS – by writing a dynamic introduction into sync grabs or pictures – it is mostly (but not always) written during the edit process. It links structural story points in the edit by writing into and out of important sync, introducing actuality, or jumping our story geographically and in time. Hence, we discuss this important aspect of multimedia writing further in Chapters 9 and 10.

Ivo's Tip: Take an interview grab that makes sense and choose a section that won't make sense unless you write specific words into it. Now practice writing in and out of that grab, so that you form a cohesive statement. What happens when you change the words?

Graphics

Graphics are often used in consumer, scientific, sporting or economic stories. But they may be used in any type of story where complex information needs to be explained. Graphics can be created on a computer, or shot with a video or stills camera, and then imported into the smartphone. They can also be recorded directly on to a camera app. Simple text-based graphics can be made in the titles section of the app's edit program.

Ivo's Tip: Import graphics quickly using Airstash or similar transfer devices (see Chapter 4).

Music

The right style of music can enhance the UGS just as if you were introducing another interesting character. Music can be imported onto iOS devices using Autofill from iTunes or from transfer devices like Airstash (see Chapters 4 and 10).

Style of Coverage

The nature and the style of coverage will impact the dynamics of the story. Covering evolving action as a sequence will help create a more dynamic feel about the actuality. Yet having lots of individual shots to edit into a dynamic montage will help create a riveting edit style. The style of coverage can act as a defining element in your story (see Chapter 5).

Sound

Last but not least, sound is the most crucial of all elements. We are willing to watch a muddy picture but we won't listen to bad sound. Where possible use a microphone as close as possible to your sound source (see Chapter 6 on sound recording). Knowing how to create a timely sound-up is crucial to making your story more filmic and emotive.

Finally, understanding the story focus or angle is crucial to creating powerful multimedia mojo-type UGS. Knowing your story is crucial to understanding *who* needs to be interviewed, which is essential to more completely developing and focusing your idea. Your first task is to decide whether your story has a beginning, middle and an end, that can be produced within the budget and schedule. The quicker you decide this the sooner you can move to the next stage, which is production or researching, an alternative story. Asking *what* is the story and *whose* story is it, will help the development process.

Not all story research happens in the office. The best and most exciting research often happens on the ground. In fact research continues throughout a production cycle. Depending on how long the piece is, research may continue to inform the story even in the edit. So as soon as you hit the ground begin seeking important local knowledge from the camel driver, taxi driver and the publican.

The *plan*, *synopsis* or *story brief* is a clarification of your idea on paper – three, five or seven points of attack. If produced early and altered accordingly, even during filming, the plan should include information on the story, characters and location, and may develop into a simple structural outline. As you become more experienced you will realize a plan is not restrictive. It's a road map to a heart-thumping, unknown world of storytelling; a non-prescriptive spine from which to branch out and come back to.

The key to any form of storytelling is to know your story and your audience, so you might consider the following checklist:

- **What is the story? The higher the stakes the stronger the story.**
- **Who are the characters and who will I interview?**
- **What about the subject matter and the resolution?**
- **What actuality will I film?**
- **What is the first impression a viewer will get?**
- **What will the body of the story look like?**
- **How will I integrate visuals, voice and graphics?**
- **When did the story happen and can I write it in such a way that makes it current?**
- **Have I used active voice in the narration where possible?**
- **How will I produce the story?**
- **My audience will want links to other information on the topic. How will I provide these?**
- **Do you know if the sites I am recommending are reputable?**

In conclusion, the old editors' truism that "when the filming stops, the filmmaking begins" is not completely true. It would be more correct to say: the filmmaking begins when you open your eyes to the world and stops on your final blink to black. In this sense your initial idea is all-important – never lose sight of what interested you in the first place – but be open to new influences that come from hanging out on those spindly branches of life.

The story will come to life on the road so don't forget all the best planning and research may change on location in some distant desert or exotic city. This is the main reason you need a plan – you can't know where you are going if you don't know where you are. You won't know where you are if you don't understand where your story has come from.

Story focus ensures you have the key story moments that create compelling storylines. It also ensures you ask your interviewees that defining question and that's what we discuss in the next chapter.

REFERENCES

Burum, Ivo. 1994. "Birth and Single Parents." In *Home Truths*, edited by Ivo Burum. Australia: ABC TV.

Harrower, Tim. 2010. *Inside Reporting*. New York: McGraw Hill.

McKee, Robert. 1999. *Story: Substance, Structure, Style, and the Principles of Screenwriting*. London: Methuen.

Stubbs, Liz. 2002. "Ken Burns: Emotional Archaeologist." In *Documentary Film Makers Speak*. New York: Allworth Press.

CHAPTER 8

MOJO INTERVIEWING

Stephen Quinn

SUMMARY

Many aspects of good interview practice remain constant regardless of the form of journalism. But mojo interviews involve some new skills and techniques. This chapter covers those new approaches, and also breaks the interview process into stages so newcomers can easily learn how to conduct powerful interviews.

A mojo interview is a form of multi-tasking, in the sense that you are shooting and listening and composing questions all at the same time. So you need to be on your toes and you must be comfortable with using your equipment so you can concentrate on the interview. But ultimately the key to powerful interviewing is your willingness to listen to the person being interviewed.

Traditional television has trained audiences to expect high production values. A television news crew will ensure that video and voice make sense and are of high quality. Mojo video interviews must also be of high quality because audiences are demanding. The big difference is only one person conducts mojo interviews, so it can be hard work.

The images and sound must be clear. Only when the news is sufficiently compelling, such as exclusive but grainy footage of a major event, will audiences make allowances for poor-quality footage. An example from recent history is the images of the Space Shuttle exploding soon after launch.

For most videos, the mojo working alone has to work hard to ensure quality, and must consider a range of responsibilities. That is what we mean when we describe mojo interviewing as multi-tasking.

An interview performs much the same role for television and the web. Its job is to get good quotes and allow the talent to express their opinions and beliefs succinctly and elegantly.

Interviews come in two basic forms. The most powerful is the on-the-spot interview with the person who has just witnessed something significant – the person who happened to be at the scene when news happened and is available to describe it. They have important information because they are witnesses. Your job is to give them the chance to describe what happened.

The other interview form is the static conversation with a spokesperson for an organization or cause or company. This is more stylized and tends to be more formal.

Within these two forms we have several types or styles of interview. These include the walk-and-talk, the impromptu and the sit-down. The type depends on the situation in which the mojo finds themselves, and the kind of atmosphere they are trying to invoke.

A walk-and-talk, as the name implies, allows you to conduct a conversation with the talent while moving through a scene. For example, you might film an interview with a garden enthusiast as you both walk through their beautiful garden. An impromptu interview, again as the name suggests, takes place when you encounter a person in a specific situation and it feels natural to do the interview on the spot, without needing to go to a studio or set up the event with appropriate lighting and background. An example might be your encountering someone with a limp, and you ask them why they are limping. What happened to their leg?

Mojo works beautifully for these two forms of interview conversation because it reflects the spontaneous nature of the interview. We see the person in their environment or we meet them in places where news has happened.

Sit-down interviews tend to be more formal and are probably most appropriate when you are interviewing the spokesperson for an organization, where you are able to position them in front of the organization's logo, or show them sitting in their office.

The type or form of interview will influence the kind of microphone you use. Refer to Chapter 6 for more about microphones. As a general rule, we use lapel mics when the person is stationary, and when in situations where you might pick up unwanted sound from the environment. When outside, a lapel mic positioned just under the interviewee's chin will help eliminate unwanted sound.

Unless you want to confront someone as part of an investigation, most of the time you should focus on using the interview to get good information. As the adage says, you will capture more flies with honey than vinegar. It is good to prepare the talent before-hand by telling them you need short answers. Explain that you do not need elegant or well-structured sentences. It's OK for them to talk in short phrases. Tell them you will probably only use "grabs" of 10 to 15 seconds, so they should aim to talk natu-rally and not try to compose perfect answers. These rehearsed answers look and sound terrible because the talent goes inside their head to repeat what they have memorized and the result is awful.

Television journalists use the word "talent" to describe the inter-view subject. What do we mean by that word? Think of yourself as a talent scout when choosing people to interview. They need to be lucid. We avoid interviewing people who stutter or who have a weird-sounding voice because we want people who make sense and who come across well in terms of visuals and sound.

Stephen's Tip: When at a breaking news event or news conference, spend some time chatting informally with any spokesperson for the company or organization. You can use the chat to gather information. The chat will also help both of you relax, and you will soon get a sense of how well they speak and how they would perform on camera.

It is OK to give the talent some idea of what you plan to ask them, though avoid providing specific questions because people will try to prepare and/or remember their answers. The result will be a stilted conversation. Give them the gist of the question before-hand, especially if the person is a newbie.

Remember, even though media is part of everyday life, the major-ity of people being interviewed by journalists have had limited exposure to the media so they will probably be a bit nervous and they will need some time to prepare. Sometimes you will tell them what the first question will be. These folk are not like professional interviewees such as politicians and business people – so it is important to make allowances for the relative lack of experience of "newbies." With professional interviewees you can be much tougher. You will need to make a professional judgment on the spot, and this is an example of the many tasks the mojo needs to perform when interviewing.

In a way mojo interviewing is like constructing a print news story. The reporter supplies the facts and background via script and actuality, and lets the person being interviewed give their opinions, beliefs, intentions, concerns, reactions and/or feelings. Think of the interview as being like the quotes in a print story. With these kind of interviews, focus on people's opinions, reactions and con-cerns. These will provide useable answers.

It helps to brief the interview subject before you press the record button, telling them what the interview will be about and asking them to frame their replies in relatively few words. In a typical news video of 60 to 80 seconds, and assuming you interview two people, each interview grab will only run about 15 to 20 seconds.

Start the interview by framing the person tightly in the viewfinder with a close-up and use your voice to introduce yourself and the interviewee and then ask the question. The reason for including your own voice is to give yourself that little boost of confidence when you start the interview through being able to have a conversation. It will help both of you to relax further. You will identify the person via a caption so make sure you get a business card to check or confirm the spelling of their name and title.

Some mojo interviews involve the reporter both asking the questions and holding the camera. This is another aspect of the multi-tasking mentioned at the start of the chapter. For beginner interviewers we recommend setting up the camera on a tripod. Frame the interviewee appropriately, tap the record button – and ensure the counter is running – and then sit down and concentrate on the person being interviewed. This allows you to focus on asking the best questions. With practice it only takes a few minutes

Figure 8.1 A GorillaPod.

Stephen Quinn

to set up your iPhone on a tripod. I recommend the GorillaPod type of tripod because the flexible arms can wrap around chairs or tree branches if they are available, or you can use it as a standard tripod. An alternative is a monopod with tripod feet. If you do not have a tripod you can often make do with something you find at the scene – a pile of books in an academic's office, perhaps, or a fence post.

Remember to listen. This is vital. Often the best questions flow from the answers to the previous questions.

Stephen's Tip: With mojo interviews aim to keep all responses short – a maximum of 60 seconds per question – to make the editing process easy and fast. If you need to ask a series of questions, break each question into a separate take rather than letting the interview run for 20 minutes. One long interview means you will need to watch 15 to 20 minutes of video to find the answer you seek if you have not noted where that perfect grab occurs. The former approach makes the editing process quicker and represents an example of how a mojo approaches the interviewing task in a different way from a broadcast television journalist.

If you prefer a new take for each question, then you will need either a remote control to stop and start the recording, or find a way to position the camera so you can reach over to press the stop and record buttons for each question. I like the option of record-ing blocks of answers because this makes the editing process much quicker. Often I do this while holding the iPhone or iPad Mini in two hands at the same level as my chin, using my body as a tripod. I can maintain eye contact with the person and get close to them. This is another example of how mojo interviewing

Figure 8.2 Stephen Quinn shows how he holds his iPhone when doing a fast interview without a tripod.

Stephen Quinn

differs from other forms of journalism. To repeat: It's much better to compose a handful of key and specific questions than conduct a long and rambling conversation – popular in the United States as a way of eliciting information. A long conversation might be fine for a print interview, but a mojo interview tends to be brief because the final product is relatively short – probably a video of less than two minutes, of which each interview grab might represent only 15 to 20 seconds. In a two-minute video you would probably interview two, maybe three, people.

Because mojo reporting is new and relatively unique, think of it as work in progress. It is OK to make mistakes. If an answer to a question is a disaster, tap the stop button, hit record again and ask the question again. You can always delete the disastrous answer later, or use the footage of the person talking and summarize their answer as a voice-over. Remember the mantra: "No failure, only feedback." Use what works and learn from that, and discard what does not work.

We believe that an interview is an intimate experience for both parties. For that reason we usually video the person we are interviewing on the same level as ourselves to suggest equality. In other words, the eyes of each person are at the same level. Avoid angles where you are looking upwards at the person with your camera. Frank Barth-Nilsen of Norway's national broadcaster NRK trains mojos in that country. "Looking into people's nostril hair isn't particularly sexy," he told me when we discussed mojo in Oslo in 2010. A downward-focused angle can sometimes be acceptable, but this removes the opportunity for eye contact that we get when interviewing someone at the same level. A downward-focused angle can sometimes seem as though you are looking down on or demeaning the interviewee.

It is important to get close so the person being interviewed so their head and shoulders fill the screen of your mobile phone. In television language, think medium close-up (MCU). Avoid filming in extreme close-up because this poses problems for name supers/captions (they end up being positioned over the person's mouth). This MCU approach reflects the intimate nature of mojo interviews. It also ensures you get good sound if you are forced to use the iPhone's microphone instead of an external mic. Speak slowly and clearly when you ask questions.

Stephen's Tip: Avoid the temptation when conducting an interview to talk back to the talent. You do not want your voice over the top of their answers because it makes editing very difficult. You can acknowledge you are listening by nodding you head. But do not talk.

Mojo interviewing in the field introduces a range of challenges. External noise can be a major problem, unless the reporter uses a high-quality microphone and/or gets close to the subject. Most of the time we recommend using an external mic. These are discussed in Chapter 6. For discreet or undercover work you obviously cannot use an external microphone. In these situations the iPhone works well without a microphone provided you get close to the person. Most discreet work will probably be done inside, so you do not encounter the problem of external or distant noise that the iPhone's built-in microphone picks up, such as helicopters, traffic or construction noise. The human ear blocks noise but the mobile phone's internal microphone captures all that external sound. It's worth re-reading Chapter 6 for advice on how to get good location sound.

Stephen's Tip: Can you put your news organization's logo on the microphone, the way broadcast news organizations announce their identity? This is good publicity for your company or website.

INTERVIEWS IN THE FIELD

When shooting outside, bright sunlight will reflect on the phone's screen. It is very difficult to frame good images if you cannot see the screen. This especially applies in a media scrum where the journalist is forced to hold the camera in outstretched arms above the interview subject. Even a small camera starts to feel heavy after several minutes. The answer here is an extension arm or monopod. See the section on monopods in Chapter 4. It also helps to get plenty of practice as a mojo before you try working in a media scrum.

With a monopod extended above a crowd, it is vital to make sure the record button is on before you hoist the monopod. Do not worry about the blurred and wasted images at the start of the video because it is easy to delete that footage during the editing process.

A fully charged iPhone might last half a day of hard mojo work. Get into the habit of carrying a recharge device and also charging your phone at all opportunities, and especially at the end of each day. BBC journalists Rory Cellan-Jones and Darren Waters, who conducted mojo trials in 2007, experimented with a range of portable solar-powered battery chargers such as the Power Monkey. But solar chargers take a lot longer than charging via a battery. And they require reasonable sunlight.

One of the problems with the iPhone is the fact the battery is built in. This means you need to charge the battery via mains power, or connect to a laptop via the USB cable, which can be inconvenient. A re-charge device is lighter and more convenient. The authors always travel with a battery charger and a recharge device. Recharging happens via the USB cable that comes standard with any iPhone or iTouch. See Chapter 4 for more details about chargers.

Always carry a charger and cable that plugs into the lighter socket of your car so that your smartphone can charge when on the highway. It is vital to have a range of strategies to deal with the worst aspect of the iPhone – its short battery life. Keep an eye on the smartphone's battery indicator. Streaming video consumes battery life quickly. Some mobile phones will beep when the battery is low. The iPad has a much bigger battery and you can get a full day's hard mojo work out of a full charge.

Stephen's Tip: Always check you have chargers before you leave for an interview.

Ideally, shoot in natural light as much as possible. If you have to shoot inside, put the subject sideways by a window (not in front of it) and use the light coming through the window. And use the rechargeable light described in Chapter 4. For indoor interviews try to find natural light from windows or entrances. Find a quiet location. It is a good idea to arrive early to scout the location to find the best place for your interviews. The microphones on many smartphones including the iPhone tend to pick up a lot of background noise. Soft materials like curtains make good interview locations because the cloth absorbs some of the noise.

Stephen's Tip: Check your audio before you do an interview. One way to save time is to ask the interviewee to tell you their name and their job title. Play that short video to make sure you have framed them well, and your sound levels are good. I use a pair of headphones to check the quality of the sound. These headphones are also very useful when editing in noisy places such as crowded coffee shops, to banish external distractions.

THE STAGES OF AN INTERVIEW

Here are guidelines for the stages of the interview process. Note that they are only guidelines, not rules. But one thing we can say with confidence: more than half of the work takes place before the interview starts.

1. **Define the reason for the interview**
    Why are you there? How long is your intended story? This will influence how much time you spend both researching and with the person. What is the target audience? Is this person the key interview subject, or a bit player?

2. **Research**

   This is the vital part of the preparation process. The aim of
   the interview is to gain good information. We do research
   to ensure we don't waste time asking irrelevant or silly
   questions. Thorough research will help you frame the areas
   you want to go into with the interviewee. It will also give
   you the knowledge and confidence to challenge muddled
   or inaccurate things your interviewee says.

3. **Make an appointment**

   Email or phone the person to arrange a time and place.
   Confirm the meeting the day before. You might need to do
   some marketing or persuasion to get them to talk with you.
   Explain the benefits of meeting you, and how the interview
   will give them the chance to give their version of events.
   Avoid use of the word "interview" because it can scare
   some people. Better to suggest you meet for an informal
   chat or briefing. Plan how you will get to the interview
   location, and allow extra time in case you get lost. Google
   Maps is very helpful for planning travel.

4. **Plan the interview**

   Plan your questions as well as your travel. Always over-
   prepare. Consider how you would deal with a taciturn
   person, or someone who talks too much. Prepare for
   what could happen if they miscalculate how long they
   can spend with you. What do you need to discuss if they
   are called away "urgently." This is a common trick among
   people who want to avoid the media but cannot because
   of their position. They get their assistant to phone them a
   few minutes into the interview with an "emergency," or they
   program their mobile to alert them to a "vital" meeting they
   must attend. All of the above happens before you meet the
   person.

   Remember to put your iPhone in "flight" mode before
   conducting any interview. This stops any incoming calls

that might disturb your interviewee. More importantly, "flight" mode stops WiFi interference. We can tell when a phone call arrives but we cannot tell if there is WiFi interference.

5. **Initial meeting and breaking the ice**

You need to prepare some icebreakers: something harmless to discuss when you first meet, such as their golf handicap or their lovely earrings. Interviews usually take place in the person's office or home, partly because people are more relaxed in familiar surroundings but also because audiences like to see people in their office or home.

Here you need to know how to see as well as look. The surroundings will often give you something to talk about as an icebreaker. If they have a photograph of themselves with someone famous, or pictures of their family on the desk, or framed degrees, you immediately have something to talk about.

6. **Establish rapport and ask your first questions**

The depth of your research shows up here. Use your initial questions to show you have done research. Once you've achieved a good rapport and you've established a working relationship, you'll probably ease into the point where you suggest where they sit as you set up your equipment. All of the above assumes you are not short of time, or they are not trying to avoid you. If they do rush away, for whatever reason, the beauty of the mobile phone is the fact you can ask your key questions without a tripod. The ethics of how this looks on camera – with the person rushing away from the interview – is discussed in Chapter 13 on ethical and legal aspects of mojo.

7. **When to ask the potentially sensitive questions**

Good rapport can work wonders, and even help you through the most sensitive range of questions. Always keep tough questions to last, unless the interviewee is rushing out of the room for that "vital" meeting. The worst scenario is being asked to leave, or the person storms off after you ask a sensitive question (though these scenarios can produce good video action). If the aim of your interview is to get good information, and you have kept your sensitive questions to the end and they storm off, at least you have the information you need. And maybe some exciting footage of the rushed exit. Another factor to consider is the non-stop talker. If you encounter this kind of interviewee, take a deep breath, count to three and interrupt with a strong question. If you interview a shy or taciturn person, you will need to find ways to encourage them to talk.

Stephen's Tip: Carry a notebook and take notes. Do not rely solely on the video as your way of recording information. An ideal notebook size fits in a shirt pocket or handbag. Or keep one in your mojo bag.

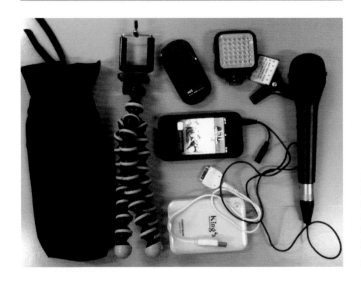

Figure 8.3 Stephen Quinn's first mojo kit that included an iPhone. Everything could fit into the black bag on the left, which originally held a small bottle of water.

Stephen Quinn

8. **How to end the interview**

If rapport is good, you may find it difficult to end the interview. You can signal your intent to close by re-examining your notes to ensure you have covered everything. Use a phrase like: "Our time is almost up. I'll just take a moment to review my notes." This is a time to ask for any documents mentioned in the interview. People will often mention reports or other materials. Make sure you ask to borrow copies of these. If they are mentioned in the interview you will need to show video or stills of those reports as B roll in your story.

Leave the door open by checking you can call back if further questions arise. Say goodbye and something like "Thanks a lot for your help." Always make sure you get a mobile number if you need to check something. Recap and check your notes for anything you may have left out. Also ask them if they have anything they would like to add.

Watch for the "after-glow." This is the result of good rapport. Some of the best comments come as you are standing at the door or lift saying goodbye. The interviewee, relaxing after the "ordeal," can sometimes offer some interesting insights and quotable remarks. The problem is you have pressed the stop button. With a mobile phone you can quickly press record and ask another question, which would be difficult with traditional equipment.

Some journalists make it a habit to ask the interviewee, as a final question, whether there is anything that has not been raised that the interviewee thinks should have been. This can be useful. By definition, your interviewee will usually know a lot more than you do about the subject. By asking "Is there anything else you think I should ask you?" at the end of the interview, it is an opportunity for them to offer useful information. Also ask the interviewee the names of other people you could speak to. By the end of the interview, the interviewee will have a good idea of the subject you are making a video about and may know useful people you have not yet come across in your research. They may sometimes give you contact details and/or open doors to potential interviewees.

Stephen's Tip: To repeat, always ask the talent where they can be contacted if you need to check anything later, and remember to get their mobile phone number and home number.

A NOTE ABOUT PLANNING AN INTERVIEW

When you plan an interview you will realize that some questions will be easy and pleasant to answer and others will not. You need to prepare for these. The well-prepared interviewer does not seek answers that merely confirm what is already known. That interviewer seeks to explore new territory. To recognize something new you have to know what's old. That's why we do research and plan an interview. Also build into your plans the likelihood of unexpected answers and surprising turns in the conversation. These provide fresh insights or new pathways to be explored, and often produce new illustrative anecdotes. Think of these things as the golden nuggets of interviewing. They come most easily to the interviewer who has planned for them.

Ivo's Tip: You cannot plan all interviews but you can be thinking about B roll as you conduct the interview. Some B roll is best recorded before the interview and as it happens. Avoid asking your interviewee to set something up when you can record B roll as it evolves.

SOME THOUGHTS ABOUT QUESTIONS

Some experienced journalists prefer not to write their questions before an interview, believing it stops them from listening properly to the answers and spontaneously asking things that arise from those answers. That is fine for experienced people, but novice interviewers will find it helpful to write down a list of questions prepared in advance that cover the key areas they want to explore. Think of it as a framework or support in case your mind goes blank, which can happen when one is under stress.

Ivo's Tip: A set of questions based on your five-point plan will help when the interview goes off track. The plan will help you work out what is relevant and how it all fits with your evolving story structure. The five-point plan is discussed in the previous chapter.

Think carefully about the way you frame the questions. Will they provoke the sort of answers and reveal the sort of information you are looking for? Remember that mojo interviews tend to be brief, so you need to get to the point quickly. This means precise and usually short questions.

Sometimes your interviewee will want to know the questions in advance. Generally this should be discouraged because it can lead to over-rehearsed replies that lack spontaneity. However, if an interviewee is new to being interviewed then a few sample questions will help them marshal their thoughts. Sometimes a useful compromise is to supply broad subject areas that will frame the discussion. Remember that even if you give a list of questions in advance, there is nothing to stop you from adding to them once the interview starts.

TYPES OF QUESTIONS

Questions fall into two general categories: closed and open. A closed question elicits a closed answer. If you ask "Can you tell me the time?" you will receive a specific and closed answer. If you ask "How do you feel about the concept of time?" you will get an entirely different response. The latter is an example of an open question. With these, the interviewee cannot give a short and specific answer but is forced by the question to elaborate on their ideas.

A closed question will generally give you a short answer that is quite specific. An open question will tend to give you the reverse. Good interviewers use both types of questions. Closed questions invite an unequivocal response. They are useful and often necessary when you need to confirm information or get someone on the record – as in "Do you still beat up your producer?" But they are less useful when you seek an expansive yet targeted response. Closed questions often sound tough, and even biased, because implicit in a closed question is the idea that it draws on or frames a limited set of responses.

How do you create open questions? The words "what" and "how" tend to be used to start an open question. Or a phrase like "Tell me about . . ." They are generally more general in their framing. Now here are some things to avoid.

Avoid double-barrel questions. These often arise when the reporter knows he or she has one chance to ask a question, such as at a crowded news conference, and so fires away with two and sometimes more questions at the same time. While understandable, these kinds of questions give the subject a choice of which one to answer. And often the subject will choose to answer the easiest or least controversial one.

Avoid statements masquerading as questions. These cheat your audience of the chance to hear answers to questions we all want to know. Remember, as a journalist you represent the public and should think in terms of what your audience wants to know. Consider all this when you plan your interview.

INTERVIEW STYLE

You will inevitably develop your own interview style and your approach will change depending on the kind of person you are interviewing, their experience with the media and the sort of information you seek. Paul Bethell, a former BBC television journalist who teaches journalism in Australia, says some journalists find that a very aggressive start to the interview can be useful in shaking the complacency of a well-rehearsed interviewee. You need to make a professional judgment as to the type of person you are meeting and the kinds of questions that are most appropriate for the start of the conversation.

But generally you may find it best to begin your interview with a straightforward question so that your interviewee relaxes and starts to concentrate on the subject in hand. It is best to leave the controversial questions until the end. As Bethell noted during a conversation in 2010: "You will have hopefully built up more of a rapport with your interviewee by then and even if your interviewee refuses to answer, you will at least have some material to work with."

Stephen's Tip: Keep your questions simple and use simple language. Questions that contain two or multiple parts and complex language can confuse the talent. They will answer one section of the question but not the other parts. Or not answer the question at all because they did not understand it.

Learn to delay your questions. Silence sometimes makes the talent volunteer information. Mentally count to three slowly before you ask your next question. Delays also make editing easier because you can easily locate the areas of silence on the audio section of the timeline.

SOME THOUGHTS ON SMALL TALK

What happens in the first few minutes of a meeting between strangers determines what happens afterwards. Some research suggests the other person sums you up in as little as five to ten seconds. The other person will use these introductory moments to size you up, and decide whether you can be trusted or mentally pronounce you a meddlesome intruder.

So the small talk with which we begin an interview is vital. It is the initial part of a bond of human communication and trust. Use of small talk identifies the conversation as a human-focused chat, not a mechanical question–answer format. In some ways you will need to play this early stage of the interview by instinct. Busy people tend to want to get right down to business and resent wasting time on small talk. Others seem to need the sense of trust and security that can be created only through the inclusion of seemingly trivial but important chat. You will need to assess every situation on its merits and then choose the most appropriate approach.

ON AND OFF THE RECORD AND ANONYMITY

As a general rule you should always aim to do interviews that are "on the record." Journalists sometimes get briefings or tip-offs on stories from official sources like the White House or Downing Street on the understanding the conversations are anonymous.

But video interviews should almost always be considered on the record. Your journalism will be more credible if it contains interviews and material from named people. Occasionally, an interviewee will ask to remain anonymous. You can show their outline but darken their face by shooting them against a window, and perhaps distort their voice. Again, you must make a professional judgment.

Before agreeing to anonymity you should consider whether the request is reasonable. Again, the judgment you will be making is whether your audience will understand why you have agreed not to identify the interviewee. It will be easier to convince them if the interviewee is discussing sensitive or personal information, or something that has criminal implications. If the interviewee is just shy or reluctant to associate their name with their comments, it will be more difficult to convince your boss or audience why you granted anonymity. The danger in these latter situations is your reader will doubt the credibility of the interviewee or question whether they really exist.

If you give an interviewee a guarantee of anonymity, you must take great care to protect this undertaking and be careful not to script anything that will reveal their identity.

Once you have done your interviews, it is often the time to edit your story. Editing is one of the magical parts of being a mojo and is the topic of the next chapter.

CHAPTER 9

EDITING ON A SMARTPHONE

Ivo Burum

SUMMARY

The art of telling user-generated stories (UGS) occurs in four stages: planning, recording, editing and publishing. The working mojo uses a smartphone to complete all four stages and in this chapter we'll take a closer look at the editing stage. This chapter covers all the important techniques used to create quality multi-track, multi-source checkerboard news-like mobile edits that include name supers, audio post-production, rendering and publishing. To cover all the material in a relevant manner I will use the iMovie app to discuss the above and where relevant will mention other edit apps that are introduced in Chapter 4.

Editors have a saying: "When the filming stops the story begins." This is so true in the mojo era because the edit happens almost immediately after the story is shot, often on location as the story is still being shot and even before that in the mojo's head, as they shoot to edit. In the era of reality TV and YouTube, two things are apparent: *story* has made way for the *event* – hey, look at this video of me eating eggs. And the high level of user-generated content (UGC) video uploaded each day – 432,000 hours – is an example of the decadence that Aristotle said would occur when storytelling dies. But is storytelling dead? Of course not, it's just in a UGC, or *user-generated coma*.

Filmmaker Ingmar Bergman summed up the storytelling and the edit process when he said, "Only someone who is well prepared has the opportunity to improvise."

Even after 35 years of working as a producer and journalist, I find improvising around evolving actuality to create powerful stories from simple ideas, is more exciting than ever. Editing footage into structure and story still feels like magic, except that it often involves very laborious preparation, creative imagination and high level editorial and publishing skill sets. It's hard work.

When I first edited pictures more than 30 years ago I was lucky enough to learn from Ingmar Bergman's editor, Ula Ryghe. She taught me the most difficult lesson in editing: she said you have to "learn to kill your babies." The more skillful you become as an editor, the quicker you will be at deciding what works and what doesn't, and you will be able to kill those shots you thought you loved. You will learn to tell stories using a quick tempo when it's required, or to slow the rhythm, to provide gravitas or emotional weight when that's needed. Here are some tips on how to begin your edit.

THE EDIT PROCESS

Once researched and shot, UGS media needs to be edited in a way that makes sense of events and transforms the edit plan into a virtual story on a timeline that's powerful and accessible. In our case this is all done on a mobile smart device. The various stages of the edit process are:

The Shoot

Being able to edit in camera, or shoot to edit, is an important skill (see Chapter 4). And the attitude that "I'll fix it in post" isn't realistic in fast turn-around mojo storytelling. Successful mojos, like all one-man band journalists, shoot the shots they know they will use in their edit. This is an acquired skill that particularly camera people working in news bureaus, who edit their own stories, learn very quickly. With practice mojos will learn to shoot only the material they need, with the odd "special" shot, and not to forget the important shots. Story coverage becomes second nature.

Ivo's Tip: Planning does not mean you don't record the unexpected; it helps determine how to use the unexpected in a story.

Viewing Footage

Scheduling time to view your footage is always important. A busy mojo will know what shots are good even before they begin their edit. They will have identified these in a small notepad, or on their smart device. It always helps to isolate good sound bites, strong actuality and relevant overlay. In a long interview make brief notes as you go. It's also important to be on the look-out for an obvious structure that supports your intended story line, or one that you hadn't planned.

Making a Rough Edit Plan or Script

Develop the story plan before your shoot and adjust it accordingly as elements develop. This plan or *story arc* comprises three major structural points: the beginning, middle and the end, with a developing point between the beginning and the middle, and between the middle and the end. This can become an edit plan that follows a story arc, which in a longer documentary program, can have as many as 13 story-development and/or edit points.

Your edit plan will include reference to sound bites, specific actuality, archive or other material that the editor might need to draw on to build the story and narration.

Choosing an Edit Method

How you proceed with your edit will depend on your experience and how you work. Here are two options:

- *Tight and right*: **This is for experienced producers, journalists and editors and the method I prefer. You edit very tightly from the start, building your narration, sync and B roll as you go. This requires deft story skill and an ability to write in and out of pictures. It is a very quick way of editing because the rough cut is very close to the fine (final) cut.**
- *The story-bed method*: **This is the way many news editors or journalists work when a story needs to be shown to a chief of staff for sign-off. This method relies on the editor putting down narration and sync grabs to create a structural bed. Reporters effectively insert the word "sync" in their scripts between paragraphs of narration. The editor, back at base, receives the film and the draft script and finds the relevant sync grabs, which are then laid up against the script. If the structure and narration works the B roll is added and the story is fine cut. This is still an effective way of working with digital media in non-linear edit suites, especially on longer current affairs or documentary formats. The aim is to get the structure right before we add B roll.**

Writing a Draft Narration

This is your first attempt at gluing story elements into story structure. Irrespective of your preferred edit option a rough narration is essential if you want to work quickly and effectively. Use the narration on audio track (A1) to lay up your vision track (V1) without worrying about overlay or B roll (V2), as per the example in Figure 9.1.

V2	Don't	worry	about	overlay	yet
V1	PTC 1		Interview		PTC 2
A1		VO1		VO2	
A2					

Figure 9.1 Example of an edit map.

Ivo Burum

The focus at this stage is writing in and out of the sound bites and not on overlay. It's preferable to work this way, to get the story structure right, before you do too much "coloring in" with B roll. The diagram in Figure 9.1 shows one PTC grab, leading into a piece of narration, which leads to a choice piece of interview sync; a pattern that creates a particular news-like story bounce, rhythm or meter.

Figure 9.2 shows a graphic representation of the above edit map after B roll has been added. In the example we are using two tracks of video and audio, which is important to enable B roll editing. The video and audio tracks mirror each other from the center out. V1 is usually where you will edit your main story element's sound grabs and so on, and V2 is where you might insert B roll to cover voice over or vision edits like those you would make when you shorten an interview. You can insert sound grabs on V2 as well. Deciding on a system that works and sticking to it is important.

The example in Figure 9.2 is known as checkerboard editing, where every second shot is placed on a different video and audio track. This is done so that you can easily replace, shorten or extend shots; something that is increasingly difficult if all shots have to be

Figure 9.2 Example of an edit map with B roll.

Ivo Burum

V2		Wide Shot		CU1&2	
V1	PTC 1		Interview		PTC 2
A1		VO1		VO2	
A2					

slotted into gaps on one track. For example, you might extend the wide shot to overlap some of the interview and do the same with CU (close-up) 1 or CU 2. This provides a more dynamic feel to your edit. But if the wide shot was on track 1, slotted between the piece to camera (PTC) and the interview, you wouldn't be able to extend it without first detaching the PTC and interview audio. This sounds complicated – and it is, which is why we work with two vision tracks: edit story on track 1 and B roll on track 2. I have left audio track 2 blank but you could add some music here.

Ivo's Tip: Changing butt edits – where edits butt up to each other – to split edits – where they overlap at the beginning or the end of the clip or shot – creates a more dynamic urgent edit feel.

USING THE SMARTPHONE EDIT APP

I felt that the best way to describe the next series of edit steps is to discuss them around an edit app. As we mainly use iMovie 2.0 I use it to describe this section (and refer to other apps where relevant), but the following edit tips will apply to any edit app. I have also included a number of videos for this section that describe the edit process and how to use iMovie 2.0.

Creating a Project

The first thing you notice with the new iMovie 2.0 is the slick user interface. Once you open it press "+," then press "Movie," choose a theme (I recommend Simple) and press "Create Movie." You will see the Home Screen and the Edit Timeline as shown in Figure 9.3.

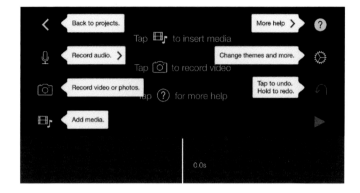

Figure 9.3 The iMovie 2.0 help screen is made active by pressing the "?" icon.

Ivo Burum

Pressing the "?" icon on the Home Screen highlights a number of dialogue boxes. These hide an array of functions that make iMovie 2.0 a powerful and intuitive app.

On the right side: "Change themes and more" allows the user to choose an edit theme. "Undo" is an excellent tool to help you return to the previous action.

On the left side: "Add media" takes you to the Library or Camera Roll where video, still and audio are chosen. "Record Video or photos" records video and photos directly into your Timeline. We recommend using either the on-board camera, or one of the camera apps we discuss in Chapter 4 and below, to record your video or stills. "Record Audio" is an excellent tool for recording narration to pictures directly into your Timeline. I record narration using the iPhone camera and then detach the audio track, because my narration is then stored with my vision in Camera Roll.

Ivo's Tip: All the iOS edit apps discussed in this chapter store video in Camera Roll, except Voddio, which stores it in a folder called "File." Voddio includes a function to import from or export to Camera Roll.

Beginning the Edit

You begin at the beginning of your story, with whatever the strongest opening element is: actuality sound bites, interview grabs, overlay with FX, music and or narration. Use a PTC if the journalist is in the thick of the action. There are two aims when starting an edit: begin with something dynamic like a great grab, or an exciting piece of vision, which creates a momentum that helps establish your story bounce; second, don't get bogged down with finessing the edit too early.

Ivo's Tip: Remember the editor's mantra "When the filming stops the film making begins," so wait until the story's right, then make it tight.

Choosing Media

Tap the Add Media icon to go to the Camera Roll to choose video, photos, audio clips or detach audio from vision clips to use as narration. Scroll up and down to reveal the clip you want. You choose media (in this case video) by tapping a clip, before dragging the yellow vertical bar at each end of the clip (the handle) to the desired

Figure 9.4 **iMovie media import icons.**

Ivo Burum

in or out point of the clip. The chosen portion of clip can be played to check that it's exactly what you want, before being imported.

A dialogue box appears offering a number of powerful options that make this app a very fast news-friendly tool:

- **Down arrow drops the selected clip into your time line.**
- **Side arrow plays the selection.**
- **Picture on picture icon drops the selection in as B roll.**
- **Picture in picture inserts the shot into another shot.**
- **Final split icon creates a split screen.**

Ivo's Tip: non-linear editing (NLE) is non-destructive. If you import too little or too much you can extend or shorten the clip in the timeline simply by dragging each end of the clip left or right. This is because the vision in the Timeline is not video but computer language – ones and zeros.

Starting the Edit

It's always a toss-up deciding how to begin the edit. If you start with a PTC you might then add a narration piece that leads into a sync grab. If you don't cover the narration with vision and you are using iMovie 2.0 you'll need to add spacer or a filler shot over the narration. I always keep 20 seconds of black spacer vision in my Camera Roll. But I also always cover my narration with B roll before I move on. Next, insert the sync grab that follows the narration. For example, insert a PTC, then narration, followed by covering B roll, then sync and so on (see Figure 9.2). Extend the beginning of your sync (sound down) left along the time line over the narration to act as spacer.

Another method is to lay down the sync and the B roll before recording narration live against the pictures. In some edit apps you can watch a series of images while you read and record live narration. You speak and record a section of script as you watch the images play through. This is a post-sync tool used often in drama and natural history. It is like radio with pictures and we don't often use this method in television where we are more concerned with actuality, which is augmented by narration. Using this method, if you are not experienced reading to pictures, you may rush the narration in your desire to match words with pictures. What may be required is to change or extend the pictures or narration. Figure 9.5 is a graphic representation of the first two options using iMovie 2.0.

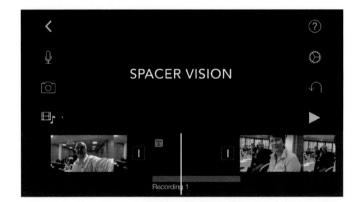

Figure 9.5 Narration with spacer.

Ivo Burum

Figure 9.6 Narration with B roll added immediately.

Ivo Burum

Creating Story Bounce

I usually edit quickly to lay down a rough narration bed as fast as possible. This helps me understand my story and to find my story bounce, which is the rhythm of the story as it bounces between narration, sync, actuality and five to seven structural points. It's best to fine tune narration after laying down a series of narration and sync sequences to enable you to listen to the statement you are creating with the narration: sync plus narration equals bounce. This is called *writing in and out of pictures* and once learned is a very useful editorial, compression and expansion skill.

One of the dangers in NLE is that everything happens too quickly. In the old analog days video spool time gave the journalist some think time. Today a journalist needs to be more prepared when working in a digital edit environment, especially when the edit is done on location, and on a mobile. If the journalist is not prepared, the danger is they spend the day trying edits, instead of completing sequences.

The way to work in any digital edit suite is to prepare well and get the story bed down as quickly as possible. Once the story is structured on the timeline the parameters are set and the structure becomes obvious and more manageable. This workflow is important for mojos who work alone and may not have another pair of eyes to look at their work.

Ivo's Tip: Structure a story to answer what you expect listeners' questions might be in the order they would arise, this will create a structure and story bounce.

Using B Roll

Supplemental footage intercut with the main actuality, or an interview grab, is called B roll, overlay, or a cutaway. It covers an unwanted zoom, a whip pan, jump-cuts and mistakes in shooting. For example, cut away to B roll of what a person is talking about while the A camera zooms in, then cut back after the zoom is complete. B roll is used mostly to cover edits where unwanted material has been extracted, like a camera zoom. Hence it is used to compress and expand sequences.

When recording an interview or a sync grab, make a note of what the person is saying. For example, they might mention an important picture that has been made into a stamp, which they own. In this case your B roll might include that picture, the stamp and even a sequence with the person looking for the stamp in an album.

When you arrive at a location and you see your interviewee – in this case the stamp collector – doing something relating to your intended interview, record this actuality even before you record your interview. For example, you might arrive at the stamp collector's shop, where he is serving a customer. Seek permission and record a sequence of that actuality, which can be used as B roll. It may not happen again while you are there.

It's a common mistake to think that B roll is only used mute. Where possible and allowable use B-roll audio at a low level to add texture to the sequence. B roll can also be used for short sound-ups during narration. These might last a word or two in between carefully spaced narration, and will add texture and a sense of the real to the piece. In television B roll is often given to broadcasters for publicity purposes.

In iMovie 2.0 inserting B roll is very simple. Position the playhead in your timeline where you want to insert B roll. Go into the Camera Roll. Choose the section of a clip by tapping and dragging the

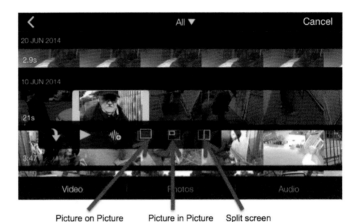

Figure 9.7 **B roll icons in iMovie 2.0.**

Ivo Burum

Picture on Picture   Picture in Picture   Split screen

yellow bars to the "in" and "out" points, then choose the Picture on Picture icon. You can also chose the Picture in Picture or Split Screen icons and even change your selection in the edit timeline. We have included a "How to Use B Roll" video at this link: www. focalpress.com/cw/burum.

Here's a few tips about how to shoot B roll:

- **Establishers – when you arrive at location shoot an exterior using a nice wide shot.**
- **Entrances and exits – shoot your subject moving in and out of a scene as this might be an interesting way of introducing them with narration.**
- **Use the lens – a wide lens is used to establish a scene and a long, or zoom lens, can pack a scene and create depth of field or composition layers, by making the foreground and or background out of focus.**
- **Actuality – try and make the B roll as actual as possible; for example, answering the phone, making coffee or selling stamps to a customer.**
- **Shoot first – if you spot something shoot it and ask questions later. Shoot the evolving action and then**

move in for a quick question. It's not a problem to quickly ask the subject to "lift the stamp again" as long as you don't slow the actuality.

- **Specials – after you have shot your primary cover shots or B roll look around for something unique that we call a "special" shot.**

Ivo's Tip: When you think you have enough B roll shoot some more.

Narration

Write your narration script and read it into an external microphone plugged into the smartphone. You can use a third-party recording app (see Chapter 4). One option is to record narration directly into the edit app. My advice is that if you want more control over your narration and still want to work fast, record the audio into a camera app and then detach it.

Ivo's Tip: Narration can be recorded reasonably quietly without boom while sitting in a car.

One major role of narration is to help compress long waffley sync dialogue and to bounce the story forward. Narration is the key tool used to compress, expand and to segue between story elements and structure. Narration does this by relating to the outgoing pictures – the overlay and B-roll pictures that cover narration – and introducing the next piece of sync or actuality. This is called "writing in and out of pictures."

When writing narration you can work on three words a second, which is the speed that we generally read at for television. So if your piece of edited video is seven seconds long, you only need a maximum of 20 or 21 words of narration. This means when working to a deadline and writing blind you can create your script on the fly by timing your pictures (video) to get a word length.

The scripting before pictures method enables a more discerning use of narration. For example, running narration for a few seconds before cutting to a powerful sound-up (lifting the B-roll sound), then dropping the sound and running more narration. In essence you choose moments, even throughout the narration, where the images do the work. The result is more filmic and less like radio with pictures.

Ivo's Tip: Narration shouldn't say what the sound bite is saying. It should lead into the sound bite and form a sentence, or one cohesive thought, which drives story from one structural point to the next.

Here are some tips for writing and recording narration:

- **Speech is more informal so write English as it's** *spoken*, **not as it's written.**
- **Write in the** *present* **tense and use** *contractions* **(as we all do when speaking) and, for news, make your audience feel as if events are happening now.**
- **Use mostly simple phrases and sentences – one idea per phrase or sentence. Sentences should be about 8–20 words. The occasional medium-length sentence is OK to provide variety.**
- **Write simply and clearly so that your aged relatives will understand.**

- **Read from a clean script when recording narration and if you use hand-written notes write them in a different color to make them easier to read.**
- **Try not to hold the paper your script is written on; use your hands to help create your rhythm while reading the script.**
- **Always read your script aloud like you are telling someone a story, not reporting.**
- **Don't inflect every second or third word, like a newsreader, only those words you would naturally emphasize.**
- **Avoid words that are difficult to sight-read (for example, communiqué).**
- **Remember that the first few words are often not heard, as the audience tunes into the story. Stephen Quinn calls these "waste words." Because UGS are visual an option might be to start with a visual and/ or audio cue to grab the audience. I might begin with a dynamic picture or sound grab, a car horn or vicious dog bark, to get the viewers' attention.**
- **Dates: Write dates on scripts the way you'd say them.**

Edit Styles

Many people who edit on a smart device for the first time use edit apps with only one vision track. This means their edits are mostly butt edits, where one shot finishes and the next begins. Working with two vision tracks will result in more dynamic edit possibilities. For example, splitting edits so that one shot overlaps another is like a car with a dual clutch. The overlap is pre-emptive editing, like getting a gear ready in a car. An example of split editing is shown in Figure 9.8. The wide shot has been extended to cover part of the PTC, the interview and

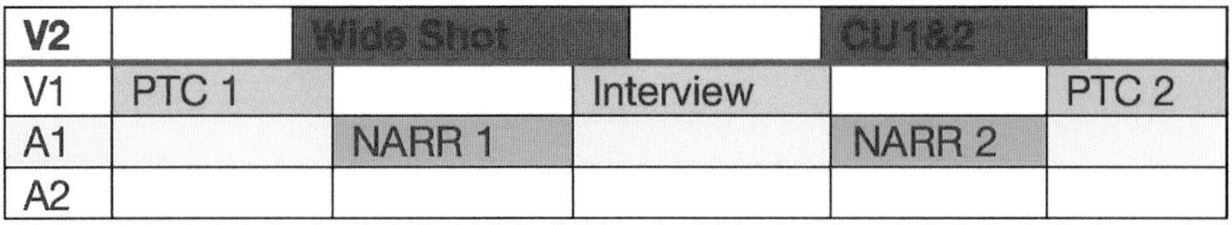

V2		Wide Shot		CU1&2	
V1	PTC 1		Interview		PTC 2
A1		NARR 1		NARR 2	
A2					

Figure 9.8 Overlapping or split edits create more immediacy and dynamics.

Ivo Burum

the narration. This creates a much more urgent and dynamic feel about the edit.

Fine Cut

Once the edit is in a rough form it's time to begin the fine-cut stage where the edit is finessed. The steps I use at this stage are as follows:

- **Go back and listen to the edit.**
- **Don't change anything at this stage.**
- **Make notes about what you feel at each section.**
- **Go back to the beginning and start fine cutting. This may require:**
  - **shortening shots so that there is no dead air after someone finishes talking;**
  - **ensuring that words aren't clipped;**
  - **slightly sliding shots left or right in the timeline;**
  - **adding B roll or replacing existing B roll;**
  - **in some cases you might need to record the narration again.**

When your story is not working on the timeline it is generally because there are redundant shots in the sequence. Go back to the beginning and watch the edit again. The point where the story fails to move forward is generally where you need to edit. More often than not, the fix is to remove footage.

> **Ivo's Tip: If it doesn't move the story forward –
> emotionally, structurally, dynamically – it shouldn't
> be there.**

Insert Name Supers and Subtitles

This is the finishing stage of your picture edit and will generally give your story a professional look. All the edit apps mentioned in this book have titles or a name super function that includes templates. However you might be instructed by the organization you work for not to add name supers, or you might be given a graphics template for your name supers.

A couple of conventions apply when using name supers. Titles tools work by inserting name supers from the beginning of a shot. Because a name super needs to appear when a person speaks, a shot needs to be split when the person talks, to create what is effectively a new shot beginning.

Figure 9.9 **Supers shot split.**

Ivo Burum

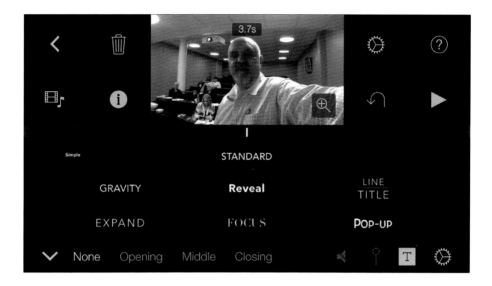

Figure 9.10 **Super styles** screen.

Ivo Burum

A one-line name super or subtitle generally appears on the screen for two or three seconds. A two-line super can stay up for four seconds or more. The general rule is that name supers appear when a person speaks and only when they are in a mid-shot (MS), medium close-up (MCU), or tighter. A good test is to keep a name super-up for as long as it takes to read it one and a half times at normal reading speed, which is about three words a second. A "How to Create Name Supers and Subtitles" video can be viewed at this link: www.focalpress.com/cw/burum.

With iMovie 2.0 press Video/Titles to reveal screen. You can see the shot has been split and the cursor positioned at the beginning of the new part of the shot. Pressing the "T" icon reveals a series of name super options. Follow the prompts.

The Title tool is used in exactly the same way to create subtitles – splitting shots to create an in- and out-point where subtitles pop on and off.

Mix and Duck Audio

The iMove, Voddio and Video Pad apps include audio mix (raising or lowering shots' overall audio level) and ducking (the ability to lower or raise audio at specific points of the timeline) features.

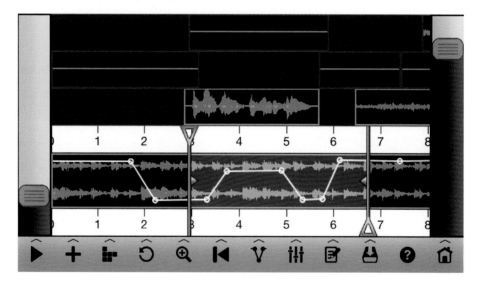

Figure 9.11 **Audio ducking on Voddio.**

Ivo Burum

Audio ducking in the Voddio and Video Pad Apps is via key frames and is very precise. In iMovie 2.0 audio ducking is more complicated and is achieved by splitting shots at the point you want to duck before lowering the level and fading the in- and out-points.

You will find a "How to Mix and Duck Audio" video at this link: www.focalpress.com/cw/burum.

Render the Timeline to Video

The final step before publishing your video is to render the virtual story on your timeline into a video. You have the choice of rendering in the resolutions shown in Table 9.1.

Table 9.1 Various resolution capabilities on a number of edit apps.

Imovie 2.0	Voddio	Cute Cut	Video Pad
1920 x 1080 (16:9)	1920 x 1080 (16:9)	Low Quality	1920 x 1080 (16:9)
1280 x 720 (16:9)	1280 x 720 (16:9)	Medium Quality	1280 x 720 (16:9)
960 x 540 (16:9)	1024 x 5 76 (16:9)	High Quality	1024 x 576 (16:9)
640 x 360 (16:9)	640 x 4 80 (4:3)		640 x 480 (4:3)
	640 x 360 (16:9)		768 x 576 (4:3)
	480 x 360 (4:3)		854 x 480 (16:9)
	480 x 270 (16:9)		

Video Pad also enables the user to choose between .mov and .mp4 file formats, plus a variety of frame rates that include NTSC, PAL and Film.

The 640 x 360 size is a standard YouTube resolution and is still used for quick uploads. The 1920 x 1080p is regarded as HD1 and 1280 x 720 is HD2. You might render and upload your files in one of the lower resolutions to get them online fast when working to a deadline. Your news editor will probably tell you that s/he will *upload the higher resolution file later*, but they rarely do, because even low resolution is acceptable on the Internet. But this may all change as we move more to web TV.

Ivo's Tip: Camera shoots in HD so your edit project
is HD. Render the project in HD and also in a lower
resolution for faster upload.

In closing, get to know your edit app and all its functions. While learning make duplicate copies of your timeline and re-edit your story using another structure to see the difference. Practice sharing your content and UGS between devices and platforms. You will need to create two or three short videos to master your edit app. But it will take a lot longer to learn the skills needed to edit dynamic stories. So keep practicing.

Mobile editing happens on location and this will impact the style of the story and the edit. Therefore you'll need more actuality to help create a more present and dynamic feel that's synonymous with location story recording. When the shooting style is hand held it provides an immediate news-type feel.

Editing is a way of *thinking* influenced by *ways of seeing* various states of immediate connectivity. This is particularly relevant in close-quarter storytelling like mojo, where the immediate is an essential story component. It is based on a state that has been described as fluid. Writer and art critic John Berger makes this observation: "The relationship between what we see and what we know is never settled" (1972: 7). Yet in doing journalism we work to settle perceptions. In this context mojo praxis, and especially editing skills, work as a filtration system to help make sense of the flowing relationship between separate unsettled realties. You will only learn to bridge these by making as many videos as you can. When you want to augment those videos you'll need to take them into post-production, and that's what we discuss in the next chapter.

REFERENCE

Berger, John. 1972. *Ways of Seeing*. London: BBC.

CHAPTER 10

POST-PRODUCTION ON A SMARTPHONE

Ivo Burum

SUMMARY

Post-production has always been regarded as the tech-heavy element of video storytelling. In long-form genres like documentary, or even longish current affairs features, it can take time and be resource heavy. Once only possible in multi-million dollar online post-production suites, video and audio post-production can now be completed in the back seat of a car using a smartphone and a bunch of apps. This chapter introduces the concept of post-production on a mobile device and describes when it is done, how, and what apps are cool.

When I worked in the field for current affairs programs like ABC television's *Foreign Correspondent*, I noticed that when we waited until we returned to Australia to complete our edit we often did a lot of a video and audio post-production. Vision was graded in certain spots and audio could be cleaned up more than would be the case on stories that were edited on the fly in some foreign edit suite.

If we edited on location it generally meant that we had a hot story, which was required urgently. Hence, cleaning up vision and audio on location was kept to a minimum. The irony is that, even without the level of post-production that happens during a back-at-base edit, the story edited in the field was always good enough to go to air. In one sense, a field edit gave the story added urgency, which gave it a certain news currency, or gravitas.

The main criteria in any story is the story, or the narrative. Audiences are more forgiving if the story is dynamic in style, informative and has engaging characters. While technical aspects are always important, a good story can carry a bad cut. A news organization's main focus is to create and publish stories as quickly as possible. If it's breaking news the audience will forgive certain quality issues.

Having said this, I make the point in Chapters 5 and 6 that while we shoot fast we never skimp on quality. Mojo is wrapped in strong journalism skills designed to produce broadcast-quality content and stories. Being a mojo doesn't mean being a sloppy journalist or producer. Understanding the techniques, tools and workflows of mojo is a first step to creating strong user-generated content (UGC), and forming that into even more purposeful user-generated stories (UGS).

THE MOJO WORKFLOW

Even though I trained as a print journalist, I've made thousands of video stories and programs and many television series; so my perspective is not print, radio or stills photography, it's video. A journalist's background (radio, print, TV or online) will determine their level of skills and influence their view about what's possible when producing mojo stories.

One purpose of this book is to fill in the gaps, and to discuss among other things the various mojo workflows. Knowing what's possible at each stage, including the skill sets and the types of mobile post-production tools that are required, is key to publishing stronger and more complete UGS from location.

One of the first decisions a mojo needs to make is whether shooting and finishing on their smartphone will achieve the desired result, or whether a more advanced hybrid system is required.

If long lenses are needed to film sport or animals, mojos might choose a hybrid *workflow* and use adaptors so that professional lenses can be used with a smartphone. Sometimes the job might necessitate that DSLR or video systems be used. A hybrid workflow may also be required for extended video post-production on graphics, for digital visual effect (DVE) moves and if more than six

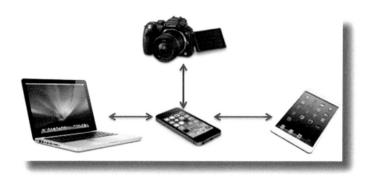

Figure 10.1 Hybrid
workflows.

Ivo Burum

tracks of audio or two tracks of video are needed when posting complex UGS or long-form user-generated programs (UGP).

Post-production is all about preparation and knowing the limitations of your gear even before you shoot a frame is important. Here are a few field tips that will help in post-production:

Recording Audio for Post

I've heard a great deal of discussion about recording multi-track audio on a smart device. Yet I'm not sure why or how to record it so that it's useful. These discussions, which are generally driven by former print or radio journalists, can have a very techno determinist approach to mobile journalism. I think this is because print journalists may not understand digital workflows and radio journalists are probably used to working with multi-track audio equipment. Solutions that suggest using break out or transfer boxes, like the AR 101, only split incoming signals so individual levels can be mixed. The result may be two tracks in, but it's still one file of combined audio out, unless you record separate audio tracks onto a multi-track App (like n Track, or Voca Live) on your smartphone. But even then the result will be two tracks combined on one file, unless you are able to save (output) each track as a separate file. Which is what is required in order to have two separate audio tracks in the edit. What we might need are split tracks recorded on a multi-track app that can be sent as separate files.

225

Do you need two tracks of incoming audio on a mobile device? Well, maybe. But reality suggests that because mojos often work alone and quickly they might find it difficult to find the time to create complex audio set-ups. Mojos need to know how to get clean audio fast. More often than not this will mean being in close to the source and using the right microphone (see Chapter 6).

If you want true two-track audio where you can post-produce tracks independently try using a Zoom H1 or H5, or another third-party digital recorder in addition to a microphone plugged into your smart device. The result will be two separate audio files (one on each device). The track from the zoom is transferred to a separate audio track on the video app, which is then synced to vision (if you require sync audio). It's a bit of work and if that level of control is needed – hey, why not. But is that real mojo work, or advanced audio recording?

What might happen in audio post on a smart device is editing out unwanted noise. The odd ping or unwanted car noise between or in audio can be removed using the edit function and B-roll cover shots. This can be done on location during post-production, sitting in the back seat of a car, wearing headphones.

Recording Narration

Recording narration is a key post-production phase, which in mojo can often happen on location. When I worked on travelling current affairs television series we often recorded narration somewhere in the field, using a car, or two pillows or mattresses positioned in a "V" with blanket to baffle unwanted noise.

Mojos will mostly record narration during their edit. This will often happen on location using either the on-board microphone, or a third-party shotgun or lapel microphone. In some cases there might be time to take the story into a more formal post-production

Figure 10.2 The narration-recording interface on iMovie 2.0.

Ivo Burum

session with access to a studio microphone – my choice is the Apogee MiC or the Rode NT-USB (see Chapter 4).

The process for recording narration directly into the iMovie app is described in the "How to Record Narration" video at this link: www.focalpress.com/cw/burum.

Moreover, it's important to remember that scripting the right words in a narration piece is just as important as getting them to sound right. Always allow time to write, read aloud and rewrite narration. Narration is best recorded and laid up against pictures, as you edit, but sometimes it is recorded before the edit. This is how it was done in the days when programs were shot on film and reporters couldn't watch their interviews after they were shot. If the story was "hot" and the edit could not be done on location because the negative or reversal couldn't be processed, it had to be sent back to base, often from another country and accompanied with a script. But how were interview grabs transcribed on location? They were recorded on audiotape, and the reporter and producer would listen to these and then write the script. But at times the story was so urgent that immediately after the interview (before s/he forgot what was said) the reporter would write a series of narration pars with the word "sync" between each. The narration was tight but loose enough to work with a number of interview sync choices the editor would ultimately make back at base.

In those days we were shooting 10 min 40 second loads of film. We had to be frugal and shoot to edit. Our interviews were focused and we'd warm up the talent before we rolled. If we over-shot during an interview where talent was being grilled, they could walk in the time it took us to change the film magazine if they weren't happy.

I still use the tight narration and loose interview sync system to get the story structure on paper and onto the timeline quickly. The idea is to create a sentence, statement or phrase, using narration and the sync grab, then keep on editing right along the timeline, creating structure and story bounce as you go. As long as it's roughly right it will do at this first stage. In the next post-production run, once pictures and sync are added, fine-tune the narration and the pictures, especially the B roll and in- and out-words, to create a strong structure.

Name Supers

Name supers are used to identify a person of note speaking on camera. Name supers are usually the final phase of the vision edit, before the audio mix and the render. Generally supers will include the person's name and often their title. A mojo working in the field for a number of news organizations might upload raw footage or edited UGS without name supers. In this case a card containing names and time codes might help (see Chapter 9 for more information). The "How to Create Name Supers and Subtitles" video using iMovie can be found at this link: www.focalpress.com/cw/burum.

Figure 10.3 Video Pad audio duck and mix interface.

Ivo Burum

Mixing and Ducking Audio

Once the picture edit is done and name supers are inserted audio needs to be mixed and ducked underneath sync grabs. Edit Apps like iMovie, Voddio and Video Pad offer audio mix and ducking features (some with key-frame accuracy), which, in the right hands, will enable professional audio post-production.

Mixing and ducking are post-production phases that can be done during a picture edit and more often when it's completed. This is because you won't want to mix audio until the picture cut is set. Otherwise you'll mix more than once. Not withstanding this, I often find myself mixing and ducking while I'm doing my picture and story edit, so that I can hear certain sections better. As we mostly use iMovie, its mix and duck path is demonstrated in the "How to Duck and Mix Audio Using iMovie" video at the following link: www.focalpress.com/cw/burum.

Ivo's Tip: If you are mixing your story on location always use a headphone and keep the audio mix level at about 2/3 on the smart device.

229

Figure 10.4 **Voddio key frame and iMovie ducking interfaces.**

Ivo Burum

Recording Location Video for Post-Production

Mojo is more often than not a what you see is what you get (WYSIWYG) environment, primarily because it is field-based smartphone work. There may be no time for vision post-production on the smart device beyond a two-track vision and audio edit in the field. The trick to getting useable vision in post-production is to keep the smartphone steady during the record. Use a wide lens, have the light behind you and shoot as much relevant B roll as possible.

Questions: Do we shoot B roll silent? Never. Do we record interviews as audio only? Never. If you need to use the audio only you can extract it by using the Detach function in iMovie, or just insert the video clip and cover the unwanted vision with B roll. It is not radio, or even worse, radio with pictures. You are creating visual proof for video stories.

Once audio and video are recorded a trained mojo's options and next move will generally be determined by how the content will be used:

1. Upload raw UGC – breaking news.
2. Edit UGC into UGS and upload the finished story – online news, features and extended paywall.
3. Transfer media to a tablet, laptop of desktop for more strenuous post-production – editing, mixing and augmentation.

If a vision fix is required on location there are a number of apps that can augment media in the field. I have chosen two that I like.

Video Grade

An option that is available to the mojo between points 1 and 2 is a post-production step called the picture grade. If required, raw UGC can be graded before it's imported into an edit timeline. For this we can use a number of apps. I use the Video Grade app, which enables fine control over the image after it has been shot and before being loaded into the edit app. You can fix underexposure, grade the image color and enhance many other aspects of the shot. This is a semi professional high-end grading tool that has more than 25 different video controls including: Brightness and tones (mid, highs and shadows), Saturation (tones), Contrast, Recover shadows and highlights, Temperature, Tint, Black and White (and tones) and Vignette.

Ivo's Tip: It works on a whole shot and if you want to edit part of the shot you will have to create sub clips.

Slo-Motion Media

You may want to shoot your footage at various speeds for a post-production look and there are a number of apps that do this. I use the Slo Pro app which enables very steady slow-motion capture. Once captured, the video can be sent to Camera Roll and then on to the edit app. It can be used at the post-production stage to shoot specific footage to highlight a particular scene or effect.

DSLR Advanced Imagery

You may require special DSLR still images or video of sport or wildlife recorded on long lenses to facilitate a post-production requirement or workflow. These can be imported into smartphone edit apps via the Apple SD card reader or transfer devices like Airstash (see Chapter 4). When transferred these images should land on the iPhone's Camera Roll, its central transfer hub. If using Android devices you will need to determine where your media will land.

Extra Media

As discussed in Chapter 4, transfer devices like Airstash, or one of the SanDisk wireless media or flash drives, can be used to import media from other platforms. These drives can also be used to export smartphone media to another platform for advanced post before reimporting it.

Render Stage

Before the story is sent to a target site it needs to be turned into a video. We call this process "the render stage." Once the vision has been graded, imported into the timeline, edited, the name supers added and it's been mixed, your story needs to be rendered into a video. Until now, while in the timeline, your story has been virtual. From the moment video is imported into the timeline it's transformed into ones and zeros, or computer language, which looks like pictures. That's why your clips are non-destructive and why they can be extended or shortened in the timeline merely by dragging their in and out handles.

Video resolution is chosen at the render stage. Remember that video can be altered on the timeline as many times as you like, and the various versions of the story can be re-rendered in many different resolutions.

Figure 10.5 iMovie 2.0 target sites.

Ivo Burum

Ivo's Tip: If you have a slow connection render your story in a low resolution and send that quicker. When you have a faster connection render the story again in a higher resolution and re send it.

Edit apps will provide a number of target sites including in some cases to an FTP (File Transfer Protocol) target. The simplest way of publishing is to upload the rendered video to free accounts on YouTube or Vimeo. Once a video is uploaded it can be embedded into WordPress, or one of the other free blogging sites, where the author can write around the video. We discuss file transfer in Chapter 12.

In conclusion, post-production on a smartphone is not that different to post-production in a million-dollar suite, except you just don't do as much, because you're often finishing and publishing stories from location. Having said this you can do enough to make audio and pictures feel, sound and look like a big dollar production if you know how and what gear to use.

By far the biggest technical shortcoming of many videos and independent film is sound. The dialogue recorded on location, which in most cases is the project's only source of dialogue, needs to be clean and of high quality. If you use the right gear described in Chapter 4 and follow the audio tips in Chapter 6, you should be well on the way to recording clean sound.

Remember that splitting video and audio on the edit timeline helps hide bad audio edits and accentuates a good vision cut. Split editing as opposed to butt editing (see Chapter 9) will help make your edit more dynamic and your audio track seamless. Using the buzz or atmos track you recorded on location to create seamless transitions between audio edits will make a world of difference to your post-production outcome. Use the key-frame ducking features to lift or lower specific audio moments to eliminate unwanted noise or heighten another important moment.

A creative and dynamic marriage of video and audio in post-production is only possible if you have recorded the right elements on location. When recording audio always record with the correct type of microphone and try to use digital microphones. Always record a buzz or atmos track on location. Never record vision with mute sound, not even for B roll. You will never know when a short sound bite will be useful. Or when someone will give you that grab unexpectedly. When it comes to video, you will maximize your post-production possibilities by recording with the light, recording lots of B roll and recording lots of vibrant actuality, which will often carry a mojo story.

Follow the simple tips discussed in preceding chapters and your UGS should be of a quality to enable you to sell it to major media outlets and publish or broadcast it across many platforms and social media sites, which is what we discuss next.

CHAPTER 11

MOJO, SOCIAL NETWORKS AND SOCIAL MEDIA

Stephen Quinn

SUMMARY

The amount of video uploaded to YouTube soared from eight hours a minute in 2008 to more than 100 hours by early 2015. Yet many of those videos are poor quality or simply pointless. Mojo offers a chance for citizens and media organizations to create high-quality videos that can be put on their social media or social networking platforms of choice. Social media and social networks are thus natural fits with mojo. You can also use these tools to promote your work.

As the manuscript for this book was being finalized the world was absorbed with news that a third person had been beheaded by an Islamic State in Syria (ISIS) fighter. On September 13, 2014 video of the execution of David Haines, a British aid worker, appeared on the web. This followed an incident on September 2, 2014 when ISIS released a video that showed the beheading of journalist Steven Sotloff.

Sotloff's death came two weeks after James Foley was executed in a similar way, and the killing shown via video. ISIS said the executions were retaliation for the Obama administration's continued airstrikes in Iraq. The major social media and social networking sites immediately erupted with activity, along with the giants like Google. A search for the phrase "beheading video" on Google on September 14 produced 16.1 million hits within 0.13 seconds.

But much of the video was old and many of the links misleading. This anecdote reveals much about the relationship between UGC, the media and social networks, which is the subject of this chapter.

Major new media companies are working hard to find ways to work with traditional media, just as mainstream media are trying to understand social networks. This was epitomized in an announcement on April 24, 2014 when Facebook launched FB Newswire in partnership with news-curation company Storyful, itself owned by Murdoch's News Corp. FB Newswire (www.facebook.com/ FBNewswire) acts like a news agency or newswire, aggregating newsworthy content from around the world from Facebook's audience and inviting journalists to incorporate the newswire into their reporting.

Storyful describes itself as the first news agency of the social media age. It publishes a newswire that allows newsrooms "to quickly and accurately source breaking news on the social web." Storyful's website says that each month it delivers more than 1,000 verified videos to its partners. "We discover and deliver rights-cleared news, entertainment, weather, technology, sports and viral videos worldwide, 24/7." Storyful says it has a "global team of journalists" ready to provide editorial support and "to source, verify and contextualize videos." All videos from both services are user-generated stories (UGS).

News Corp, the Murdoch-owned global news group, bought Storyful for about US$25 million in December 2013. At the time Robert Thomson, News Corp's chief executive, described Storyful to the *Wall Street Journal* as the "village square for valuable video" and said it used "journalistic sensibility, integrity and creativity" to find, authenticate and commercialize user-generated content (UGC). "Through this acquisition, we can extend the village square across borders, languages and platforms."

At the same time Storyful's chief executive Mark Little said journalism in the age of social media needed to be "open, innovative and collaborative" reflecting the business model that would sustain it. "News Corp is a natural fit for a company which wants to help reinvent the news industry."

Based in Dublin, Storyful locates, verifies and acquires timely and relevant UGC and distributes those videos to its partners. Its tools allow customers to integrate video into their news or advertising content via online and mobile platforms and also to monitor social conversations and sentiment. As Storyful's website notes: "We clear hundreds of videos a month for web and broadcast use and have a UGC archive of over 110,000 videos. We also sell licensed videos for all types of broadcast and commercial use."

A News Corp media release announcing the acquisition said that in 2013 verified user-generated videos managed by Storyful generated 750 million views for its partners. Many major news groups such as the *Wall Street Journal* use Storyful content. By September 2014 the number of videos Storyful staff had curated on YouTube had passed the one billion mark.

Craig Silverman, writing on the Poynter.org blog in late December 2013, said Storyful's ability both to find and get the rights to UGC video, and to drive revenue from this was unique. "The other two news organizations that do a really good job of surfacing and obtaining permissions on a large scale are Associated Press and BBC, but they do not have as much of a revenue model around this practice. Storyful has that, and the video. With that in mind, spending US$25 million to get into this game at the top level looks very smart for News Corp. Plus, Storyful says it earned its first profit last month [November 2013], making it a business with a reasonable prospect of helping, rather than hurting, the News Corp bottom line."

The Storyful–Facebook partnership represents a powerful example of the potential of the interaction between social networks, citizens and journalists. This chapter argues that mojo blends beautifully with social media networks like Storyful, YouTube and Facebook, because mojo offers the best way to create quality videos. We argue that most of the video on these sites is poor quality; perhaps only about 2 percent is excellent.

When announcing the partnership with Storyful, Andy Mitchell, Facebook's director of news and global media partnerships, indicated that his company considered every Facebook user a potential partner in news. He began his announcement with: "Every day, news is made on Facebook. More than one billion people use our platform to discover, explore and participate in news-making events around the world."

In other words, Facebook believes its members create UGS and FB Newswire is the best way to link them with journalists. The site's Facebook page describes FB Newswire as "a resource for journalists" that gathers "newsworthy social content shared publicly on Facebook by individuals and organizations." It is a significant example of how the relationship between the media and citizens is evolving, with social networks such as Facebook acting as an intermediary between citizens and major media networks. Thus "newsworthy content" provided by Facebookers around the world becomes available "for journalists to use in their reporting."

Videos created on social media sites but curated by news organizations are potentially big business. The above example indicates the power of video. News Corp has clearly identified video as a key priority. Other media organizations have come to the same conclusion, as Chapter 1 noted. It is likely that other media companies will consider building their own versions of Storyful.

The Internet remains a huge photocopier, in the sense that new ideas can easily be copied and reproduced. Many media companies could harness UGC in the same way that Storyful has, especially if they adopt the ideas in this book. So mojo has a major role to play in helping citizens to create good video. An example is Twitter's June 2014 announcement that it would buy SnappyTV: "It's important for us to provide tools that make it easy for TV broadcasters, businesses, and event producers to share high-quality videos. To that end, we've agreed to acquire SnappyTV."

Social media describes the way people connect with each other by sharing videos and photographs online. Millions of people around the globe use their mobile phones for that purpose. The

Figure 11.1 **The logo of the company Ivo Burum runs, Burum Media. The authors use social networks extensively to market their companies.**

Ivo Burum

best-known example of social media is YouTube. Jawed Karim, Chad Hurley and Steve Chen launched YouTube in February 2005. The site's first video, "Me at the Zoo," shows Jawed Karim at San Diego Zoo. It was uploaded on April 23, 2005. Only 18 months later Google bought YouTube for US$1.65 billion.

In early February 2008 I interviewed a Google vice-president, Douglas Merrill, in San Francisco. Merrill said eight hours of video were being uploaded to YouTube every minute of every day, 24 hours a day. A little over two years later, on March 17, 2010, the official YouTube blog announced that 24 hours of video were being put on YouTube every minute. By May 2013 more than 100 hours of video were being uploaded to YouTube every minute, which means more than four days of video is being uploaded each minute. Figures for 2014 were not available on the official YouTube blog but we can assume the number will be higher when released.

Social networking works on the same sharing principle as social media, but people use digital tools to connect or network with each other. The best-known and biggest example is Facebook. Mark Zuckerberg founded Facebook with university roommates and computer science students at Harvard University. Zuckerberg's prep school, Phillips Exeter Academy, had for decades published a printed manual of all students and faculty, unofficially called the "face book."

Zuckerberg began writing code for "The Facebook" in January 2004, and it launched on February 4 that year. The site became Facebook a year later. Membership was initially restricted to students of Harvard College. In the first month, more than half the undergraduate population at Harvard had registered. Eduardo Saverin (business), Dustin Moskovitz (programming), Andrew McCollum (graphic artist) and Chris Hughes joined Zuckerberg on the project. In June 2004 Zuckerberg and Moskovitz moved Facebook's headquarters to Palo Alto in California's Silicon Valley. Facebook took almost four years to attract its first 100 million members – by August 26, 2008. But growth has surged since, and Facebook claimed more than a billion users in October 2012, and had about 1.2 billion by its tenth birthday in February 2014, and 1.32 billion by August 2014.

LinkedIn is not as big as Facebook but is the other major player in the world of social networks, though with a business focus. It facilitates ways for registered users to maintain a list of people they know and trust in business, and "link" with them. LinkedIn launched in May 2003. By March 2010 LinkedIn had more than 60 million registered users in more than 200 countries. By April 2014 its user base had risen to 300 million.

Twitter is probably best described as a cross between a social networking and a social media company. Jack Dorsey, Biz Stone and Evan Williams co-founded a company called Obvious that spun off to become Twitter. Jack Dorsey published the first tweet on March 21, 2006. It is a free micro-blogging service that enables users to send and read messages known as tweets. A tweet is a post of up to 140 characters that appear on a user's profile page.

It is called micro-blogging because of the limited number of characters. People "follow" other Twitter users, and tweets are automatically delivered to those subscribers. Twitter had 75 million registered users by the end of 2009. By September 2014 the number had soared to 271 million monthly active users, who sent half a billion tweets a day. Three in four accounts (77 percent) are outside the United States and almost four in five active users (78 percent) access Twitter via their mobile phone.

Twitter is more news focused than Facebook. Matthew Ingram, writing on the GigaOm blog on August 18, 2014 after the shooting dead of an unarmed African American in Ferguson, Missouri, which became a huge news story, identified the fundamental difference between the two platforms. "Part of the reason why Twitter is more news-focused than Facebook has to do with the underlying mechanics of both sites, and the way user behavior has evolved as a result. Because of its brevity, and the ease with which updates can be shared, Twitter is a much more rapid-fire experience than Facebook, and that makes it well suited for quick blasts of information during a breaking-news event like Ferguson. Facebook's environment makes it more problematic as a news source because its newsfeed is filtered by the site's powerful ranking algorithms."

In a sense, Ingram wrote, Facebook had become more like a digital version of a newspaper – "an information-gatekeeper that dispenses the news it believes users or readers need to know" rather than allowing readers to choose for themselves. "In the end, we all have to choose the news sources that we trust and the ones that work for us in whatever way we decide is important. And if we choose Facebook that means we will likely miss certain things as a result of the filtering algorithm – things we may not even realize we are missing."

Emily Bell, a former journalist who runs the Tow Center at Columbia University, pointed out in a think piece in *The Guardian* on August 31, 2014 after the Ferguson shooting that news "is now not just outside newspapers, it is outside newsrooms." It was impossible, she wrote, for humans to filter efficiently the vast numbers of images, videos, tweets and updates created and shared by humans, bots and devices. "By 2020, according to consultants Gartner, there will be 20 bn devices connected to the internet, and they will all have something to say for themselves. Facebook, Instagram, Twitter, WhatsApp and what's next are and will continue to be making editorial decisions on our behalf." Facebook's algorithm and other sorting processes were less accountable, she said.

"The decline of the newspaper, and the subsequent closure or shrinking of newsrooms, not only leaves news unbound, it also removes the culture of editorial filtering. Centuries of human debate over cultural values, expressed in everything from intrusive splashes to grandiose editorials, are disappearing to be replaced by a black box," Bell warned.

Meanwhile, the flow of videos continues. Facebook purchased Instagram for US$1 billion in April 2012. As of late 2014 Instagram had about 200 million active users who uploaded an average of about 60 million photographs a day. Most of the social media and social networking sites mentioned above focus on video. We have already described the huge volume of video on YouTube. Facebook video upload numbers are also large.

Liz Gannes reported on the GigaOm site in March 2009 that Facebook received about 415,000 video uploads a day. More recent data were not available. On October 5, 2012, Twitter acquired a video-clip company called Vine that had yet to launch, as a way to generate video (Vine launched in January 2013). Vine allows people to create and share six-second video clips. Twitter later released Vine as a stand-alone app. It is difficult to ascertain the number of videos linked to Twitter. The company's blog does not supply that information. But given half a billion tweets a day by September 2014 – or 5,700 a second – and assuming 5 percent of those contain a video link, that suggests about 25 million videos a day associated with Twitter.

This represents big money. The most popular online destinations globally are Google, Microsoft, Facebook and Yahoo! These major sites gather the bulk of the global spending on advertising. In 2013 eMarketer estimated that Google, Facebook, Microsoft and Yahoo! received 59 percent of all of the digital advertising revenue in the United States, and this group was projected to earn 61.7 percent of the same advertising pie in 2015. Between four-fifths and five-sixths of their audiences access these sites from outside the United States.

THE VIDEO AUDIENCE: UGC AND MILLENNIALS

Given that UGC is media created by one's peers, we need to consider who those peers are. Some academics have described UGC as the kind of content we should never trust because it has not been verified or produced by a professional.

A major study in 2014 from Ipsos, the global research company, refutes this belief about "millennials" (an abbreviation of millennial generation). Demographers use the term to describe the segment of the population born between about 1980 and 2000. The media sometimes refers to them as "Generation Y" or the "Internet generation." They prefer to consume video online and don't watch much television, compared with older age groups. Ipsos reveals that millennials trust UGC just as much or more than professional reviews. And UGC was 20 percent more influential than other types of media when it comes to purchasing and 35 percent more memorable. Millennials spend five hours a day with UGC, Ipsos said.

How does mojo fit with these findings? Social media are evolving and mojo is one key aspect of it because it represents a superb way to curate content. The 2014 edition of the *Global Digital Media Trendbook* maintains that targeting the millennials is the next big opportunity for media companies. The book has appeared every year since 2006.

"The most powerful ways to reach millennials are through social media, and through digital media with strong social media components," the book says in its executive summary. But publishers must speak to the millennial audience "in a profoundly different way than older generational groups," it warns.

> "Young people want to read about serious topics, but they want to hear authentic voices. They've been lied to one too many times by politicians, they've been misled one too many times by news outlets," said Jake Horowitz, co-founder and editor-in-chief of PolicyMic.com, a news website targeted at millennials. "Young people are not going to news sites. They're going to Facebook, Twitter, Instagram, Pinterest, Vine. You have to reach young people where they're having conversations," Horowitz said.

According to a study by Telefonica and the *Financial Times* in 2013, millennials are three or four times more likely to identify the Internet and social media news sources as more credible than printed newspapers and magazines, depending on the region of the world where they live, the *Trendbook* reported. And millennials were two or three times more likely to identify Internet and social media news sources as more credible than television, their study said. They are also prolific users of smartphones.

The mobile phone is a major driver of change on the Internet, as networks like 4G evolve and spread. By mid-2014 the world's population had reached about 7.01 billion, and they were using almost 6.9 billion mobile phones. Simple mathematics suggests an average of 97 out of every 100 people on the planet had a mobile device, up from 95.5 percent half a year earlier. But these averages are misleading because people in some regions own more than one mobile phone per head. But they do show the massive penetration and growth of mobile devices around the globe.

SMARTPHONES AND MEDIA CONSUMPTION

Smartphones facilitate media consumption. Half of America's mobile population in 2014 consumed media on their smartphone. In other words, more than 116 million people were browsing the mobile web that year, accessing applications or downloading content via a device they kept in their handbag or pocket.

About 1.2 billion smartphones were expected to be sold by the end of 2014, a 23 percent increase from the 1 billion shipped in 2013, according to information the analytics company IDC published on its website. About 1.8 billion units would be sold in 2018. Ramon Llamas, research manager with IDC's Mobile Phones team, said smartphone shipments would more than double between 2014 and 2018 in key emerging markets such as India, Indonesia and Russia. China would account for almost a third of all smartphones shipped in 2018.

The 2014 edition of the Reuters Institute Digital News Report, entitled *Tracking the Future of News*, edited by Nic Newman and David Levy, noted that mobile and social consumption of news was reaching "a new level of intensity." Indeed, almost half of the smartphone users surveyed for the report (47 percent) said they mainly used apps for accessing news. The report covered ten countries and noted varying demographic changes: "We see the different behaviors of young and old becoming more pronounced, and new kinds of journalistic organizations emerging."

Almost two in five online news users across all countries surveyed in the report (39 percent) used two or more digital devices each week for news and a fifth said their mobile phone was their primary access point. "Over the past year we have seen another signif-icant jump in the adoption of both smartphones and tablets for news – as consumers embrace the benefits of smaller, personal, always-on devices. Germany and France have had a catch-up year, while others like Denmark have surged further ahead with 52 percent of the sample using a smartphone for news and 34 percent using a tablet on a weekly basis."

On average more than a third of their global sample (37 percent) was accessing news from a smartphone each week and one in five (20 percent) from a tablet. This was driving more frequent access to news and from more locations, the report said. "As more people come on board, the profile of multi-platform users is getting more mainstream. Smartphone news users are getting older – we have seen a significant jump in usage by the 25–44 group – while falling prices have enabled tablet use to spread to less affluent groups and to the young."

ADVICE FOR NEWSROOMS

Newspaper newsrooms that focus on print need to wake up. Most people have already learned about the news when they read it in the printed newspaper. The future is multi-media, especially video on the web. So every reporter – indeed, every person in a news organization – should know how to shoot video.

That includes the delivery truck drivers and the security guards and the staff in the canteen. These people should be trained to capture fast, raw video with their iPhone and these unpolished clips can be posted quickly from the field. A second group of highly skilled video journalists should produce more sophisticated video stories, perhaps using digital SLRs instead of iPhones. Stories should either be raw, fast and prolific, or considered and well constructed (like small well-crafted documentaries). Either way, mojo is the best way to achieve this goal.

As Brian Storm of MediaStorm.com says in the Tow Center report: "There's two things that are really successful in the space that we're in right now: being really, really funny . . . or the highest-quality thing that you've ever done. . . . Those are things that people tweet, those are the things people post on Facebook, right? The stuff in the middle, the volume, is noise."

LENGTH IS IMPORTANT

Given the power of UGC video, what is the ideal UGS length? Short videos remain the most effective way to attract users and increase traffic on news websites. When I ran the video section of the *South China Morning Post* we mostly insisted that reporters keep news videos under 70 seconds. If a news site is going to offer longer videos, they need to be of very high quality.

Building a capacity for video news online remains an exercise in faith, claims a report from Columbia University's journalism school published in April 2014. Despite the fact that videos do not directly produce revenue, they still have an important role to play in a news organization's business strategy. They act as the "point of entry" for many audiences. The report, entitled "Video Now: The Form, Cost, and Effect of Video Journalism," was published by Duy Linh Tu for the Tow Center for Digital Journalism at Columbia University. For now, experts advise publishers to work out how to do video well and think about revenue later, the report said.

The authors of this book believe that mojo offers a powerful model for making videos because consumers and editors want complete UGS as well as raw UGC. It is about quality, not quantity. The other factors are the ability to use social networks to alert audiences to that quality, and focusing on niche markets.

Social media and social networks combined with mojo is a formula for success. Most videos on YouTube get fewer than a few thousand views because they are either poor quality or the audience does not know they exist. News organizations need to engage new audiences through social networks. Reach out to them on platforms like Facebook, Instagram and Vine. Before they can do that they need to learn how the users of these platforms think and relate to the world.

Here is an example of a video niche market. On August 16, 2013 News Corp launched BallBall so football fans in Indonesia, Vietnam and Japan can watch match highlights on their mobile phones and online. News Corp claims a combined market of more than 460 million people. CEO Robert Thomson said football was "the ultimate global sport in an era of globalization and digitization." All content is available in local languages. News Corp holds the exclusive English Premier League mobile and Internet rights in Japan, Indonesia and Vietnam through to the end of the 2015–16 season. BallBall shows highlight clips, including every goal from England's Barclays Premier League. BallBall represents an example of how media companies are exploiting video in a range of ways.

MOJO BUSINESS MODELS

Much has been lamented in recent years about the death of mainstream media, as we watch thousands of jobs disappear in the West (though media continue to prosper in Asia). Yet the world's universities continue to produce hundreds of thousands of graduates. Where are the jobs for them? Graduates with mojo skills can establish small production houses. The equipment, as discussed in Chapter 4, is very inexpensive compared with the cost of making television a generation ago.

The issue for these new small companies will not so much be the quality of the stories they produce – because we know mojo can create quality videos. The issue will be making the world aware of what has been produced. This is where social networks become vital. Graduates need to know about social networking tools to be able to market and promote their business. They will also need skills in running a small business such as organizing spreadsheets and databases. The opportunities for mojos are only limited by one's imagination.

Videos made with a smartphone involve large files. The next chapter talks about the need to manage the files on your smartphone so you always have available space to shoot video when the situation arises.

CHAPTER 12

FILE DELIVERY AND PHONE MANAGEMENT

Stephen Quinn

SUMMARY

Videos that mojos create tend to be very large files. This chapter covers the routines and practices needed to send these files successfully from the field. It also shows how to maintain your iPhone or iPad so your device does not become clogged with too many large digital files because we cannot shoot video if the device's memory is full.

It used to be said in California that one could never be too thin or too rich. For mojos we need to add a phrase to this epigram: "Too thin or too rich, or have too much memory on your mobile phone or tablet." A skill that mojos need to embrace when using their iPhone for "full mojo" is file management. Shooting video in the field generates a lot of large files. These files will soon occupy most of the space on your phone's memory unless you establish routines for creating space on your device: This means moving files from the device to some sort of storage location, or when necessary deleting files. This situation can happen even if you choose an iPhone with the largest hard drive (64Gb for the iPhone 5 or 128Gb for the iPhone 6) or an iPad with the largest memory (128Gb).

Mojos need to set up a regular regime to move or delete unnecessary files. This should happen at least once a week. It can be done anywhere – on a bus, train or taxi, or while you are enjoying a coffee break. It can even happen in bed. If you do not introduce these regimes, your phone will get sluggish and you might find you cannot record a vital piece of actuality because your phone's memory is full. By the time you delete files to make enough space to record something important, the chance to shoot that significant event will have passed. Remember the Boy Scout motto and be prepared.

> *Stephen's Tip: Develop a routine of plugging your iPhone into mains power as you prepare for bed at night. This is also a good time to do your data management as part of a weekly routine. These habits will serve you well in the world of mojo. You clean your teeth before bed. Think of these tasks as essential mojo digital hygiene.*

If your company supplies the iPhone or iPad you use to make videos, insist on the largest possible memory on the device. Some news organizations are overly careful with money and supply the cheapest device. This means the iPhone or iPad with the smallest memory. Ultimately this is false economy and a stupid practice. Both authors have worked with or consulted to companies that purchased the cheapest devices. It was painful to listen to reporters complain about problems associated with hard drives that soon became full and unusable.

> *Stephen's Tip: An ideal situation is to carry two iPhones, though this is not always possible. If your company supplies an iPhone with a small memory, thank them. Then buy yourself a back-up iPhone or iTouch or iPad. Because Apple introduces new devices each year, more and more pre-used mobiles and tablets become available fairly cheaply at places like eBay or in second-hand shops.*

VIDEOS ARE LARGE FILES

We have mentioned elsewhere in this book that all edited HD videos made with an iPhone and iMovie involve large files. As a general rule, think in terms of at least one megabit (1Mb) of data for each second of video. Thus a minute of mojo video will be at least 60Mb. Mobile phone networks in some countries issue a warning when you try to send a file via 3G or 4G larger than 20Mb, and suggest you use Wi-Fi. Given most videos which journalists create with iMovie will run at least a minute, you will need to carry a Wi-Fi device at all times. It is frustrating and pointless creating the most newsworthy or exciting video in the world if you cannot send it to your office or file to YouTube.

A PRIMER ON BITS AND BYTES

We need here a short discussion on the different kinds of data used in computer and mobile phone networks. A "bit" is the basic unit of information in digital communication. The word "bit" is a contraction of "binary digit." The encoding of text via bits was used in Morse code and other early digital communications machines such as teletypes and stock-market tickers. Digital information flows as electrical pulses that are either on or off. Think of it as a light switch: the switch can either be on or off. It is usually described a "1" or a "0" indicating that status of being on or off.

Historically, a "byte" was the number of bits used to encode a single character of text in a computer. Thus eight bits are generally said to make up a byte. Werner Buchholz coined the term "byte" in 1956. He deliberately chose to spell the word that way so it would not be confused with "bite" because that word was too close to the spelling of "bit." When abbreviated, a "bit" is designated with a lower case "b" while a byte has an upper case "B." Thus one megabit is 1Mb and one megabyte is 1MB.

Figure 12.1 The rapid spread of the Internet around the world has produced a visual blight: hundreds of cables. This image from Bangkok, the Thai capital, is less visually awful than in many other cities.

Stephen Quinn

Silly fact: Four bits are known as a "nibble" or "nybble" (based on the notion that a nibble is a small bite). Presumably this is an example of digital humor.

We now enter a discussion about the terms needed to describe the amount of storage in a digital device such as a mobile phone. Mojos need to understand the language of digital memory. In the metric system, a kilo denotes multiplication by – or a factor of – 1,000 and is abbreviated as a "K." Thus one kilogram is 1,000 grams and one kilometer is 1,000 meters. In terms of digital storage, a kilobit is 1,000 bits and is written Kb.

Mega in the metric system denotes a factor of a million. Mega comes from the Greek word for "great" and is abbreviated as an "M." Thus in a digital camera a megapixel means 1,000,000 pixels. In terms of digital storage, a megabit or 1,000,000 bits would be abbreviated as 1Mb.

Giga denotes multiplication by – or a factor of – a thousand million. The word comes from the Greek for "giant" and it is abbreviated as a "G." It is sometimes written as 10 to the power of 9 – that is, 10 with 9 zeros after it. So when we read that a mobile phone has a storage capacity of 16 gigabits, or 16Gb, it seems like a lot of capacity. But because video files are so large, over time that capacity fills and in a worst-case scenario you cannot shoot video because there is no space left on your hard drive.

We also hear of digital storage expressed in terms of bytes, such as a megabyte (MB) or a gigabyte (GB) or a terabyte (TB). As the size of digital files increase, and the flow of digital data across the globe soars, we need even bigger concepts to indicate the amount of data. A terabyte consists of a billion bytes, a petabyte is a thousand billion bytes, an exabyte is a trillion bytes, a zettabyte is a thousand trillion and a yottabyte is a billion trillion bytes.

GROWTH IN WORLDWIDE DATA FLOWS

In June 2014 Cisco, the company that designs and makes much of the world's networking equipment, published its global Internet traffic forecast. Video would represent 79 percent of all consumer Internet traffic in 2018, up from 66 percent in 2013. If we include other forms of video such as Skype and video on demand, video traffic could represent up to 90 percent of global consumer traffic by 2018, Cisco said. Internet traffic via mobile devices would grow significantly by 2018 and represent almost an eighth (12 percent) of total Internet traffic by 2018, Cisco noted.

Information released at the 2013 Mobile World Congress in Barcelona confirmed that mobile growth would mostly be driven by data usage rather than voice. In 2012 the volume of data transmitted through mobile devices amounted to 0.9 exabytes a month. As noted earlier in the chapter, 1 exabyte equals 1 billion gigabytes. This was more than all the data transmitted in all previous years combined on mobile phones. By 2017 data transmission is expected to reach 11.2 exabytes. A major contributor to the boom in data transmission will be a huge growth in video streaming, analysts said, predicting a surge of 75 percent in the four years to 2017. Deployment of 4G networks will be a major factor, as people enjoy faster upload speeds.

These kinds of concepts are difficult to comprehend. You do not need to understand these huge numbers, but you do need to ensure you have enough space on your mobile's memory to be able to record large video files. The message here is to be consistent and keep the memory of your smartphone free of clutter. Become a tidy mojo!

REGULAR ROUTINE

At least once a month, open the Camera Roll on your iPhone and/ or iPad and delete as many unnecessary files as possible from the previous month if you do not have somewhere to save those files. In this case you might need to be strong, even brutal. The photographs and videos you used last month are probably no longer relevant for the news you will cover today or this week. A better option is to employ an external storage device such as an Airstash, SanDisk Connect Wireless Media Drive or Sandisk Wireless Flash. These transfer files between the iPhone and the storage device via Wi-Fi and are described in Chapter 4. The SanDisk comes with 64GB of on-board memory, while the amount of memory on the Airstash depends on the size of the SD card you insert. When fully charged these devices can run for more than seven hours and stream to several mobiles at the same time.

News is ephemeral. Once you have filed your news video today, you will move on to the next assignment. It makes sense to keep your files for the previous month on your device, in case any questions arise. After a month the likelihood of queries will diminish so it's safe to store the files elsewhere. If you believe you might re-use some video footage for another story, then it is even more sensible to invest in the portable storage devices described in the previous paragraph. These have become relatively inexpensive compared with their cost a decade ago, and are available from most electronics retailers.

The nature of news means that generally all videos and stills you used for today's news item would have been taken today. It is relatively easy to add video to a story given that most of the time you will be reporting from the scene of the action. With iMovie it is very easy to grab some extra footage with the iPhone straight into the iMovie app from the scene as you create your video.

The advantage of having two iPhones – one for work and one for personal stuff – is you can keep the photographs and videos you are nostalgic about on your personal mobile. But the one you use for work must have sufficient space for shooting a range of videos at short notice. This means you must check often to ensure available space, and delete or transfer files as part of a weekly or monthly routine.

Stephen's Tip: Some frugal news organizations – and I have worked for one of the most cheapskate newspaper groups in Asia – might insist on reporters sharing iPhones. In one instance the newspaper required reporters to delete files and hand over a virgin phone when the reporter went on vacation so someone else could use the device. Resist these stupidities. This is another example of false economy. Every reporter should have an iPhone supplied by the company, and that iPhone should have the largest possible memory. If you find yourself working for a cheapskate news organization, the best option is to buy the device you use for reporting, rather than rely on your employer supplying one. You can always claim it as a legitimate business expense when you pay your taxes. And you have the comfort of knowing you do not need to hand the mobile to another person when you go on vacation.

FILE MANAGEMENT

Once you have completed editing your video you should save it to the iMovie Theater. Think of it as a back-up. The beauty of this approach is even if you delete files accidentally, you have a completed version of your video to send to the newsroom or put on YouTube or Vimeo. You should save to iMovie Theater as soon as possible after you have finished your video. If you try to save after you have deleted files from your Camera Roll you will get a warning message "This project contains clips which have been deleted from your photo or music library" and you will not be able to save to iMovie Theater. So make saving to iMovie Theater *straight after* you finish a project a part of your video-making routine.

YOUTUBE VERSUS VIMEO FOR SHOWCASING

Use YouTube or Vimeo to store your completed videos. Think of it as your personal showreel – the place where you showcase your best work, and refer potential employers to when looking for a job. Which do we recommend? I believe YouTube is the better option because it is owned by Google and therefore very unlikely to be shut down. It offers lots of options for improving your uploaded videos, and because Google owns it you can use various Google social media tools for telling people about your latest project. A YouTube account is also free.

Vimeo also offers a free option but frankly it is nowhere near as good as the professional version. The latter costs £159 or about $US270 a year as of late 2014. Vimeo gives priority to people who file to the professional version so if you use the free option you will often find yourself waiting in a queue behind the people who have purchased the professional version. And sometimes the wait can be long. It is likely the $US270 fee – that was the price as of late 2014 – will rise in years to come because when I started using Vimeo's professional version in 2011 the annual fee was only $US65.

YouTube's vast size means that people will find it difficult to locate your videos, given the huge number of videos uploaded every minute. This has the advantage that if your video is unique, it is not likely many people will find it, so your news stories will remain exclusive. You can always designate your video on YouTube as private, so that only you and your producer know how to access it.

If you do want to publicize your videos, you will need to spend time using social networks and social media to let people know you have released a new video. Read more about this in the previous chapter. As of mid-2014, people were uploading 100 hours of video onto YouTube every minute, according to YouTube's official statistics page. Other interesting facts from the site: more than 1 billion unique users visit YouTube each month, more than 6 billion hours of video are watched each month on YouTube (that's almost an hour for every person on Earth) and 80 percent of YouTube traffic comes from outside the United States.

Once your video has been uploaded to YouTube or Vimeo, phone your producer at the office to let them know the video is available. You can either make your video public, which is the simplest option for sharing, or you can make it private to stop your opposition from monitoring your achievements. If you choose the private option you will need to give your producer your account password so they can get access to your videos.

Once your producer has access to your latest video they can copy the embed code and paste that code into your company's content management system (CMS), or any blogs you use for distributing news and information, and then publish your story. It is easy to embed a video and then copy and paste in a CMS. Select the relevant video in YouTube. As it plays you will see the "share" option in the menu below the video. Click once on share and another screen will appear. You will see the word "embed." Click once and you see a box of text (it's actually HTML, the language of the web). Copy that text and paste it into your blog.

All blogs have two formatting options when you create an item: "visual" and "text." The former is like a word processor and allows you to make text bold or underlined. The latter "text" option consists of HTML. You should paste the video's embed code into the HTML or "text" option because most content management systems require you to paste code into the HTML. Once you have press save, the video will appear in the blog post.

FILE MANAGEMENT IN iMOVIE

It is important to establish a routine for removing completed video files from iMovie because these completed projects are large files and these files will ultimately clog up your mobile device or tablet. We suggest once a month you spend some time checking inside the app to see what can be deleted or sent to an external storage device. Remember, once you save your completed video to iMovie Theater you will always be able to find that video in the Camera Roll of your iPhone or iPad. Ensure you give it a memorable name.

File management is important when working as a mojo. We tell you this so you will never experience the embarrassment of having no space on your mojo device when trying to shoot an important scene.

Now that you have learned about file-management skills, we move to the next chapter to consider the important ethical and legal aspects of mojo work.

CHAPTER 13

ETHICAL AND LEGAL ASPECTS OF MOJO

Stephen Quinn

SUMMARY

This chapter also covers important and relevant legal issues such as privacy, defamation and trespass. Mojos need to know how to stay legally healthy. That is the aim of this chapter. Working as a mobile journalist introduces a range of ethical and legal issues that print reporters do not always encounter. One of the most dangerous is the urge to file quickly if that desire for speed overrides the process of sound and ethical decision-making. A mojo needs to devote time to developing a moral compass so they are prepared in advance for a fast-paced world.

Mojo's speed creates lots of potential issues and dangers. Modern apps and smartphones make it possible to make and send a story to the newsroom in minutes. As anyone who has driven a fast car knows, anything that involves speed involves risk. And the higher the speed, usually the higher the risk.

This chapter suggests we need to appreciate and arrange appropriate ethical frameworks before newsgathering starts, to prepare storytellers for the fast-paced world of mobile journalism. We need to be prepared before we press the record button because everything thereafter happens so quickly. Other issues to be considered in this chapter include privacy, trespass and defamation, and the role and influence of citizen mobile journalists.

All humans encounter ethical dilemmas. Journalists face more of those dilemmas than most people. Daily journalism sometimes means daily dilemmas.

Hourly journalism – such as working with social media or online or creating mojo videos – creates even more issues. The speed of mobile journalism intensifies some of those issues because by the time we correct an error or apologize for an ethical breach, the story has probably moved on well past the point where those errors or breaches can ever be resolved.

Two key issues that need to be appreciated are the ease with which it is possible to film people without their knowledge, and the speed with which stories get onto the web before journalists have time to consider the implications of those stories. We repeat, whenever speed is involved it is vital to prepare citizens, students and professional journalists beforehand with an adequate moral compass.

Thus, as the speed of newsgathering and UGS accelerates on the web and in social media, ethical training becomes more important than ever. Reporting almost "live" accelerates the potential to make mistakes and to commit ethical blunders. Editorial executives should hold critique sessions soon after journalists have completed mojo assignments to allow for feedback about ethical consequences.

Matt Cowan, a former broadcast journalist with Reuters, was one of the people involved in the mobile journalism trial Reuters instigated in 2007. These trials are described in the first chapter. Cowan commented on the ease with which he could work discreetly as a mojo:

> As someone who is used to working with a big camera, this is a different kind of experience. It fits in your pocket. What's amazing is that you can sidle up to someone and take pictures and video, which people find surprising. It has real potential to capture people's thoughts in places where you would not have a full crew. Its portability is what makes it so exciting.

The new technology would ultimately help broadcast journalists, Cowan said, because it was less intrusive than traditional cameras and microphones.

I encountered the issue of ethical questions when I worked as a mojo in Australia in 2007. At the time mojo was an unknown form of journalism. I attended a news event organized by a football club's media minders. A star player in the Australian Football League was scheduled to make a statement to the media, answer a few questions for the media scrum to keep the television news crews happy, and then return inside to the clubhouse. In Australia this is called, in media slang, "feeding the chooks [chickens]."

Under no circumstances, the media minders said, would individual interviews be allowed. I walked alongside the football player as he returned to the clubhouse, and streamed live video back to the website of the local newspaper. The football player probably thought I was taking stills because we see people taking photos with mobile phones all the time. I introduced myself as a journalist, but this might have been lost in the hurly burly of the moment. The point is, with mojo it is very easy to shoot video when people are not aware that the video camera is running.

In some respects, mobile journalism is a reflection of society and its changing mores and values. For example, the rise in the number of mobile-phone cameras has led to a surge in the amount of dodgy video content sent to the web and accessed on mobile phones.

In most cases people have used mobile phones to upload content to the web. Much media comment has focused on the high levels of pornography and related ethical breaches associated with how easy it is to shoot stills and video anywhere. Let us look at some prominent examples.

In March 2011 Taiwanese actress Barbie Hsu married mainlander Wang Xiao Fei on Hainan Island off China's south-east coast. The couple asked guests not to take photographs or shoot video. Yet Charles Zhang, CEO of Chinese Internet search company Sohu. com, used his mobile phone to blog about the wedding. Zhang and other guests provided a "virtual live telecast" of the event delivered to blogs via their camera phones. In a statement after the wedding Zhang described his action as "no big deal," adding, "I stopped when I was told to. I don't think I have done anything against the law or wronged my friends. So I will neither admit to any wrongdoing nor apologize." He said he wanted to record the joyous occasion for Hsu's fans and interested members of the public. "Prior to the dinner party [where guests were reminded not to take and upload photographs], I really did not know we could not take photos and put them on our micro-blogs," Zhang wrote. All content about the wedding was subsequently deleted from his blog.

The groom, Wang Xiao Fei, told a different story on his own blog. He wrote that he was angry when he discovered that Zhang, a friend and business associate, had brought an employee from his search engine's entertainment section as a guest to film the event.

"I really regret inviting Mr Zhang to my wedding," Wang wrote on his blog. Journalists from across Asia hung around for days at the wedding venue, but missed getting video because of Barbie Hsu's media restrictions. They reacted angrily when they discovered Zhang had covered the event. Taiwan media in particular criticized Barbie Hsu for her perceived favoritism towards the Chinese media.

The issue here is not about allegations of favoritism but the ease with which citizens with mobile phones can shoot video discreetly. Another example from China demonstrates a trend occurring in many parts of the world: pornography on the web delivered via mobile phone.

In Beijing, in February 2010, a famous Chinese model was involved in an Internet sex video scandal. Zhai Ling, also known as Shoushou, received considerable bad publicity when videos of her performing sex acts appeared on the Internet. Her former boyfriend allegedly shot the videos.

Shoushou had a promising modeling career after being named top model at the Beijing Motor Show in 2008. The Chinese media reported she was the subject of a range of negative stories because of the videos. Those videos were still available on the web as of late 2014. Shoushou's career went downhill afterwards, even though the person or people at fault posted what was presumably private material on a public place – the web.

The incident demonstrates both how easy it is to film with a mobile-phone camera and send the video to the web, and the destructive consequences for people's lives and careers.

These incidents highlight a major change brought about by mobile phones equipped with a camera. The mobile phone makes recording so discreet that many people do not know they are being filmed. Because mobile phones are small, unobtrusive and unthreatening, some people do not believe they are talking to a camera and, in turn, potentially to millions online. As American blogger Jeff Jarvis has written: "Life is perpetually on the record."

UPSKIRTING

The phenomenon of "upskirting" where (presumably) men take videos or stills of women has grown significantly in recent years. People position themselves under department-store escalators, for example, and post that video on the web. Others find ways to take photographs of women using hidden cameras such as devices secreted in their shoes.

A Google search for the term "upskirting video" in June 2014 produced 292,000 results in about half a second. The term "upskirting" has evolved so that it now refers generically to any voyeur photography that involves taking an image of somebody in a private moment or location when the person does not know the image has been taken.

PRIVACY

Many countries do not have laws to protect a person's right to personal privacy, especially in a public place. The legal position varies considerably. In Australia, for example, all states have passed laws making it illegal to take "upskirt" photos in public places without the subject's consent.

In India, section 66E of the Information Technology Act punishes anyone who publishes or transmits the image of a "private area" of any person without their consent – with up to three years in prison and/or a fine not exceeding about $US4,000. In Japan, hidden-camera photography is not against the law but distributing those photographs publicly may break the law. Camera phones sold in Japan generally make a noise when taking a picture, making the subject more likely to notice if "upskirt" photos are being taken.

In New Zealand it is illegal to make a visual recording of a person's "intimate parts" when the person has a "reasonable expectation of privacy."

The United Kingdom has no bans on taking such photographs but the activity could be prosecuted as voyeurism under the Sexual Offences Act 2003 or as outraging public decency. The United States does not have any specific legislation that forbids "upskirt" photography and videography.

But the Video Voyeurism Prevention Act of 2004 punishes people who intentionally make an image of an individual's private areas without consent, when the offender knew the subject had an expectation of privacy.

Upskirting is one thing. Mojos are also likely to encounter ethical issues related to violent images and the notion of taste.

One of the earliest examples of a challenging video taken with a mobile phone involved the death of 27-year-old Neda Agha Soltan, shot dead on June 20, 2009, allegedly by Iranian security forces during a protest against claims of corruption in the presidential election that year. Someone named "Mohammed" filmed her last moments with his mobile phone and put the video on his Facebook account. The video circulated in Iran and around the world, and stirred wide outrage in a society infused with a culture of martyrdom. Opposition websites and television channels, which Iranians viewed via satellite dishes, repeatedly aired the video, which showed blood flowing from her head as she lay dying. From there international media picked up the video.

The CNN version of the story had almost two million views on YouTube as of late 2014. The video can be seen at www.youtube.com/watch?v=b5KBrsz1oxs (warning: the video is graphic). Neda's name became a rallying cry for Iran's opposition who protested against what they claimed was an Islamic dictatorship.

Elsewhere in the region, the "Arab Awakening" in Tunisia began in December 2010 after another incident captured by an amateur mojo and put on Facebook provoked widespread alarm. On December 17, 2010 a young fruit and vegetable seller, Mohamed Bouazizi, burned himself to death after police confiscated his merchandise and local authorities stopped him from working. The video, taken with a mobile phone, was picked up from Facebook and re-broadcast repeatedly on social media and television throughout the region and the world.

TASTE

Taste depends on our moral decency. Ivo Burum believes we need to make sure we have treated people decently and that we do not use offensive material that is culturally insensitive. Basically the story needs to be made in good taste, so that everyone can watch it. But this will always be a fine line. In his television work he used his family as a barometer when it came to making a decision about taste. Would my mum watch this without squirming? While taste is arbitrary, societal conventions can help guide our work.

These events involving Neda Agha Soltan and Mohamed Bouazizi represent examples of the changing relationship between new and traditional media. Mobile phones are the most common communication device around the world and citizens can use the apps described earlier in this book to create powerful news reports.

Mojo work has never been the province of only the professional journalist. It is available to anyone who invests in the technology and training, and who has the opportunity to record video in a newsworthy situation. Traditional media organizations need to work out how to work with citizen mojos. This is discussed at length in Chapter 2.

ETHICAL CONSIDERATIONS

What are the ethics of showing video of the bloody death of an innocent student, or a man who incinerates himself as a protest? Is it fair to show Neda's last minutes on film? Or the burnt body of Mohamed Bouazizi?

Journalists – who belong to professional organizations – probably follow that organization's code of ethics. But not all journalists – especially freelancers – are members of professional bodies. And citizens who create user-generated stories (UGS) probably do not belong to any professional associations. Any code of ethics beyond a professional code will be a personal code, and that code will vary from culture to culture. It is impossible to comment on individual codes of ethics for journalists.

This means journalism educators and people who train citizen mojos need to ensure thorough training in ethics for all types of aspiring journalists. And media organizations need to provide regular briefings and updates on ethical issues for their staff. All ethics training must happen before people begin reporting – think of it as being supplied with a moral compass. Given the speed at which news happens with a mobile phone, it is impossible to think about ethics as one is pushing the record button.

Mobile- or cell-phone journalism offers opportunities and dangers. The opportunities include the almost instant transmission of video, stills and sound. We have numerous examples where mobile-phone footage has captured newsworthy events.

The dangers are linked with the opportunities, and they are often the same ones that have existed since the Internet became widespread. These include the problems of who is monitoring what goes onto the Internet, and its accuracy.

Until recently, professional journalistic standards were connected to institutions – now those standards are often detached from such institutions. Two decades ago these institutions were the curators of the news; now they are less in control. Social media has developed its own structures and values.

Technology has a dark side as well as a silver lining. Heather McLean, writing in the Smartchimps blog (www.smartchimps.com) on June 11, 2014, noted the unprecedented levels of wiretapping carried out at mobile-phone networks around the world. On June 6, 2014 Vodafone issued a report acknowledging that 29 countries in which it had networks had received a lawful demand for help from a law enforcement agency or government authority between April 1, 2013 and March 31, 2014.

Vodafone said government agencies in those 29 nations had implemented their own technology on the Vodafone network or carried Vodafone's data traffic through their own systems so they could tap calls directly. This report highlights the fact that governments around the world tap into people's conversations when they deem it necessary, even though many individuals believe those actions are not appropriate. The human rights advocacy group Privacy International expressed deep concern and said Vodafone's report highlighted an area that required even more transparency from operators, governments and businesses.

One of the best-known recent examples of the use of mobile phones and small digital cameras in repressive regimes is the documentary *Burma VJ: Reporting from a Closed Country*. Anders Østergaard directed the film that follows the September 2007 uprisings against the military regime in Myanmar, formerly known as Burma. Much of it was filmed on mobile devices, and the footage smuggled out of the country. The video has received more than 40 awards around the world, including the Sundance Film Festival's prize for best world cinema documentary, and the top prize at the International Documentary Film Festival in Amsterdam, in 2009. In 2010, it was nominated for an Academy Award for Best Documentary Feature. You can watch the video online, and find more about the film, at http://dogwoof.com/films/burma-vj/.

As well as images of the suppression of public protests in Myanmar in September 2007, in recent years the mobile phone has provided news organizations with video of many major news events. These included the hotel shootings in Mumbai in November 2008, the aftermath of the Iranian election from June 2009, riots in Urumqi in north-western China in July 2009, the tsunami in Japan in early 2011, and more recently the pro-democracy "Arab Spring" uprisings in a range of Arab nations in 2010–14.

When protests and riots occur, many repressive regimes throttle the speed of the Internet so that broadband becomes slower than dial-up. But it is considerably more difficult to control mobile-phone networks because the mobile phone is the main tool for business, especially in developing nations. In some countries, authorities have contingency plans that involve closing much of the mobile-phone networks if protests get too large.

This certainly happened in Iran after the country's disputed national elections in 2009, and during the Red and Yellow Shirt protests in Thailand in recent years. But people still capture video on their mobile phones and find ways to distribute the video using social networks such as Facebook or YouTube, or mailing or hand-delivering the mobile phone or its memory cards across borders.

CITIZEN MOJOS

Research shows the most frequent creators of mobile-phone video are people aged under 30. In most countries in Asia, apart from Japan and South Korea, huge proportions of the population are young. In Cambodia, half of the country's population is aged under 20. In Indonesia a quarter (27 percent) of the population is younger than 14; in Malaysia it is 29 percent. In the Middle East, more than 60 percent of the population is aged under 25. The "Arab Spring" uprising in the region from late 2010 has been directly connected to a combination of young people using mobile-phone cameras and social networking tools such as Facebook. The penetration of personal computers in the Middle East is low, but millions of people have mobile phones, and they know how to use them for political impact.

> As a journalist based in Hong Kong between 2011 and 2013, Stephen Quinn often travelled to nearby Macau to do stories. More money is gambled in Macau than in the United States and the United Kingdom combined. But Macau's casinos forbid people from shooting stills or video. After being thrown out of three casinos, Quinn discovered the power of discreet apps on his iPhone such as TS Video (TS stands for top secret). The lite version is free and the pro version costs about US$1. When filming the app displays a custom image that looks like a browser window, or email program, or e-book – so when security guards accuse you of filming you can claim you were merely browsing the web, checking your email or reading.

LEGAL ISSUES

As we have already established, technology makes it possible to film and distribute video quickly and widely. Journalists need to understand the laws as they relate to shooting and transmitting video. This necessitates a thorough knowledge of defamation law, and related laws of privacy (discussed earlier) and trespass.

Defamation

When producing stories it is very important to know the difference between what can be said and shown about someone and what cannot. In other words, you need to know what is defamatory. Libel and slander are subsets of defamation and are discussed in the next paragraph.

This section is not a substitute for further study of the laws that affect mojos. At all times we are bound by the laws of the land. For example, you cannot speed just to get to the scene of a story more quickly. Some laws are specific to the work of reporters. You should familiarize yourself with media law and definitions in the places where you will be working.

Any living person or entity, except a corporation or government body, can bring an action for defamation. (With the dead, exceptions exist where the estate of the deceased can sue.) Defamation is a published and false statement that damages someone's reputation or holds them up to ridicule in the eyes of their peers.

To establish a case, the plaintiff needs to establish that material was published to at least one person other than the plaintiff and the defendant (easy to do given the reach of the Internet), that the material was defamatory and that they were identified. The defamation can come from the words and images individually and collectively in the total context of the publication. In some countries slander is defamation that is spoken, and libel is defamation that is published.

One of the difficulties in working within defamation law is the potential range of interpretations. So it's very important to know the defamation laws in your country or state. Here are a few tips to get mojos thinking about the implications of defamation. We have also highlighted a number of myths about defamation, and given you the reality.

- **Myth: Defamation laws serve to restore a person's damaged reputation. Reality: Once damaged, a reputation is rarely restored and damages are a way of compensating for this fact.**
- **Myth: Defamation makes a mockery of press freedom. Reality: Press freedom relies in part on**

practicing good journalism and this means staying within the bounds of defamation law.

- **Myth: Journalists don't get sued for defamation, only their publications do. Reality: Not true.**
- **Myth: I'm protected if I quote someone else making a defamatory statement. Reality: Not true, but in some situations and in some countries, such as reporting from Parliament or the courts, journalists are protected by "privilege."**
- **Myth: I'm safe if I give both sides of the story. Reality: Not true.**
- **Myth: Accidents happen and it was an honest mistake. Reality: Ignorance is no defense.**
- **Myth: It is OK to publish the truth. Reality: Yes, but proving the truth is often difficult. Not only must you know it's the truth, but you must be able to prove it in court.**
- **Myth: Poor people don't sue. Reality: While legal aid is not available to bring a defamation action, some lawyers will work on a no-win no-fee basis.**

A way to avoid defamation is to make sure all information you have is correct, and that you can prove it is true. It is important that you give the person you are commenting about the right of reply.

Here is a checklist:

- **Is the statement true?**
- **Does it discredit someone?**
- **Is it published? (It will be in the case of mojo stories because of the Internet.)**
- **Does it identify the person?**
- **Has the journalist been negligent or deliberately tried to defame someone?**

Stephen's Tip: As a journalist you should keep your file notes for as long as possible, but at least for 12 months. Check the rules in your jurisdiction.

More on Privacy

The law assumes everyone has the right to privacy (though interestingly, a bit over a century ago there were no privacy laws). This means mojos need to know when and where they can film.

In most countries it is legally acceptable to film in public locations, but not in private places. If you film on private property without permission you commit trespass. But confusion exists as to what defines a public place. A city street is obviously a public place. So presumably is a beach or a park. But when does a city street end and a private house or block of apartments begin? At the door? At the gate? On the verandah or balcony? Many people spend time in shopping malls and car parks. Is a shopping mall or a car park a public place?

Another problem is the fact that the law of trespass varies from country to country. Canada, for example, has no uniform approach to the issue of trespass, which means journalists need to familiarize themselves with the applicable federal, provincial, territorial and city statutes. Canada's Criminal Code does prohibit trespassing at night.

A journalist found loitering or prowling on the property of another person near a private residence can be found guilty of trespass. If charges are filed against a reporter, the burden of proof falls on the journalist to prove they had permission to conduct their business from the lawful owners of the public land.

In the United Kingdom, taking photographs or footage on public streets and roads and also adjoining private land where permission to shoot has been granted is not considered trespassing. But "trespass to goods" refers to picking up a document or object without permission and photographing or filming it.

And "trespass to the person" refers to a camera crew compelling a person to be filmed without their consent by stopping the person from getting into their home or place of work. Trespass is not usually a criminal offence in the United Kingdom and, for this reason a police officer usually cannot threaten an arrest for civil trespass.

The exception relates to specific laws covering sites such as Ministry of Defence property and establishments that prohibit photography. The Criminal Justice and Public Order Act 1994 created the criminal offence of aggravated trespass. Section 69 of the Act gives a police officer the power to order any person believed to be involved in aggravated trespass to leave the land. If a person refuses to leave, this is regarded as an offence.

Aggravated trespass carries a penalty of up to three months in prison. A possible defense for journalists, photographers and film crews who fail to leave the land in question is that they could under the Act have "a reasonable excuse" to stay – namely to cover the event. But journalists have no guarantee this defense will stand up in court.

In Australia, journalists do not have special rights to enter someone's property beyond that of an ordinary citizen. Reporters are liable for trespass if they enter land or premises without the owner's permission, except when they are in the process of seeking permission.

Journalists can also be liable for trespassing if they put a listening device or a camera on someone's property without their permission. A journalist can visit private or business premises and "doorstep." This refers to groups of journalists staking out territory near a newsworthy event or property and waiting to film people when they leave the property. The safest place to enter is the public area of a business such as the reception because the public has an implied invitation to call.

Reporters have no right to be on private property. The consent of the owner or tenant to enter and stay is required, and the journalist must leave when asked or directed to leave by the owner or tenant. Once someone is asked to go, any implied public invitation ends.

Reporters often turn up on private property in situations such as fires, disasters, demonstrations and protests on the basis of an inferred invitation. The extreme inferred invitation is a television "walk-in" – entering premises with the camera running – and it invites ejection with reasonable force under trespass laws.

In Australia a public street is the only place where journalists have unlimited rights of access but these rights can be limited when police close a road. Entry to parks and controlled public areas requires observance of relevant by-laws.

In the United States, a reporter can be sued for intrusion when they gather information about a person in a place where that person has a reasonable right to expect privacy. Newsworthiness can be a defense to this kind of invasion of privacy.

Reporters are generally allowed to enter privately owned public places such as school campuses or malls. But they must leave when asked. As well as trespass, another common type of intrusion involves secret surveillance – that is, using bugging equipment or hidden cameras. Laws vary in each American state but as a general rule reporters can legally photograph or record anything from a public area, such as a sidewalk, but they cannot use technology to improve upon what an unaided person would be able to see or hear from that public place.

The American Civil Liberties Union (ACLU) notes the citizens, including journalists, have the right to photograph anything that is in plain view when the citizens are lawfully present in public spaces. This includes taking footage of federal buildings, transport facilities and the police. "Such photography is a form of public oversight over the government and is important in a free society," the ACLU website says.

When you are on private property, the property owner may set rules about the taking of photographs. If you disobey the property owner's rules, they can order you off their property (and have you arrested for trespassing if you do not comply).

Police cannot confiscate or demand to view photographs or video without a warrant.

If you are arrested, the contents of your phone may be scrutinized by the police although their constitutional power to do so remains unsettled. In addition, it is possible that courts may approve the seizure of a camera in some circumstances if police have a reasonable, good-faith belief that it contains evidence of a crime by someone other than the police themselves (it is unsettled whether they still need a warrant to view them).

Police cannot delete a citizen's photographs or video under any circumstances, the ACLU says.

Police officers may legitimately order citizens to cease activities that are truly interfering with legitimate law enforcement operations. Professional officers, however, realize that such operations are subject to public scrutiny, including by citizens photographing them. Note that the right to photograph does not give you a right to break any other laws. For example, if you are trespassing to take photographs, you may still be charged with trespass.

As we can see, laws relating to trespass vary considerably from country to country. This means journalists need to research and learn the laws related to the countries where they work.

As this book was going to press, a landmark decision in the New Zealand High Court defined a blogger as a journalist. The ruling has given legal weight to what is already becoming a reality in the media landscape in many parts of the world. In an appeal against a defamation case brought by businessman Matthew Blomfield against Cameron Slater (founder of the Whale Oil Beef Hooked blog), the court found that Mr Slater could be legally defined as a journalist.

The decision hinged on the definition of Mr Slater's blog as "news media." In his appeal Mr Slater said: "The rules . . . do not say you have to be this massive corporate. My website has broken numerous stories . . . I deal with informants and sources and people who want to provide confidential information on a daily basis." In delivering the court's finding, Justice Raynor Asher said:

> Mr Slater's reports contain genuine new information of interest over a wide range of topics. While criticisms can be made of Mr Slater's style and modus operandi, Whale Oil is not of such low quality that it is not reporting news.

Things to Consider

The law is complex. As a mojo you need a good working knowledge of laws that affect the way you work. You cannot claim you didn't know. Forgive the cliché, but it's always better to be safe than sorry. Heed Ivo's advice:

> As a mojo you should always try to be accurate; make sure your story is designed to minimize unwarranted harm; be compassionate and sensitive; respect privacy and a person's right to a good name; make sure you have the right permission to film and encourage people to have their own say.

The next chapter offers a range of videos, web links and articles to improve your mojo knowledge. The section on media law is most helpful.

CHAPTER 14

MOJO RESOURCES

Stephen Quinn

SUMMARY

This chapter offers a range of videos, web links and blogs designed to help journalists, teachers and students learn more about being a mojo. Each section relates to the content in the chapters in this book, in the order the chapters appear.

CHAPTER 1: MOJO AND THE MOBILE JOURNALISM REVOLUTION

In July 2014 the BBC College of Journalism, part of the BBC Academy alongside the colleges of production and technology, opened their training website to the public. In the past it was only available to people based in the UK. Its educational resources are exceptionally good. The site is open for a 12-month trial and might be available beyond that date. This article has links to three videos about iPhone journalism: www.bbc.co.uk/academy/journalism/article/art20130702112133388.

This is one of the first videos about how to capture video with a cellphone, and is interesting for historic purposes: www.youtube.com/watch?v=JpWS-6pMzwo.

Ruud Elmendorp profiles African mojo Evans Wafula, based in Nairobi in Kenya. Though made in 2007 it is useful as a historical link to mojo's past: www.youtube.com/watch?v=XxznVB0kGNk.

Readings about Mobile Journalism

Stephen Quinn's Delicious account has lots of mojo news and is updated most weeks: http://delicious.com/sraquinn/mojo

History of Mojo

Ilicco Elia talks about the tools included in the original Reuters mojo toolkit in this three-minute video: www.youtube.com/watch?v=L_OJGeamwbs.

Find other Reuters videos about the early days (circa 2007): "Reuters Mobile Phone Reporting Part 1" at www.youtube.com/watch?v=lpUMxZS6muw; "Reuters Mobile Phone Reporting Part 2" at www.youtube.com/watch?v=p1kVbvhp4lk; and "Reuters Mobile Phone Reporting Part 3" at www.youtube.com/watch?v=03SAMopg8Ww.

Video about Mojo in General

Australia's Newspaper Publishers' Association has produced an interesting video called "How to Shoot and Edit a News Video on the iPhone." It runs for almost 12 minutes and can be watched on YouTube at www.youtube.com/watch?v=Ui8087sNUEk.

CHAPTER 2: CITIZENS AND JOURNALISM

In 2013 Ivo Burum, the co-author of this book, created an excellent iBook called *How to MOJO: Guide to Mobile Journalism*. This excellent book is available via Apple's iTunes store and is highly recommended. It contains videos that show how to use a range of apps, including iMovie and Voddio.

Ivo also maintains some excellent blogs and websites. The blog CitizenMojo aims to empower citizens to be mojos: http://citizen mojo.wordpress.com.

Ivo's SmartMojo focuses on practical aspects of mobile journalism: http://smartmojo.com.

An excellent site that showcases how Ivo trained indigenous Australians from six remote communities in the Northern Territory as mojos is called NTMojos http://ntmojos.indigenous.gov.au.

Ivo also runs Burum Media: www.burummedia.com.au.

Media Organizations Working with UGC

Scoopshot helps citizens who take videos of newsworthy events sell them to media organizations: www.journalism.co.uk/news/advertorial-scoopshot-makes-smartphone-users-part-of-the-newsgathering-process/s2/a556742/.

The toolkit for CNN's i-Report: http://www.ireport.com/toolkit.jspa

The training program for Yahoo's YouWitness News: https://ontributor.yahoo.com/academy/.

Working with CBS's EyeMobile: http://treemolabs.com/work/cbseyemobile.php.

Tools for Citizen Journalists supplied by the Knight Citizens News Network: http://www.kcnn.org/tools.

CHAPTER 3: MOJO ACROSS PLATFORMS AND GENRES

Read Ivo's articles about emerging genres at http://burummedia.com.au/digital-evolution/ and http://burummedia.com.au/perfect-digital/.

CHAPTER 4: TOOLS OF THE MOJO TRADE

Vericorder Technologies in Canada have been mojo pioneers. As well as creating the Voddio app for mojo work, they have set up an online shop to sell mojo equipment: http://vericorder-outlet.com/.

Glen Mulcahy trains journalists for the Irish national public broadcaster RTÉ. His blog about mobile reporting and mojo tools is always interesting and useful: http://tvvj.wordpress.com/category/mobile-journalism-mojo/.

An interesting idea: using drones and/or balloons to get aerial shots with a smartphone. Read about Africa's first newsroom-based "eye in the sky": www.africanskycam.com/.

Amani Channel created this blog that details some of the equipment he likes to use: http://www.webvideochefs.com/mobile-gear/. The site also offers a free guide to mojo at www.webvideochefs.com/mobile.

D.J. Clark heads the multi-media department for the Chinese national television network CCTV in Beijing. His website contains a section devoted to mobile reporting: http://multimediatrain.com/?page_id=575.

The New York Times published a good piece about a new device for holding your iPhone, the iOgrapher: www.nytimes.com/2014/07/31/technology/personaltech/the-iographer-helps-improve-your-video.html?_r=0. Ivo Burum is a television producer, journalist and mojo trainer, who writes about mobile technology and has a number of how to videos at www.smartmojo.com

CHAPTER 5: COMPOSING VISUAL PROOF ON SMARTPHONES

A helpful BBC video about recording video: www.youtube.com/watch?v=YsediltYmls.

Witness, a not-for-profit site, offers a range of excellent videos about shooting video. Find them at www.witness.org/training/how-to-videos. Witness is an international non-profit organiza- tion that has been using the power of video and storytelling for more than two decades to open the eyes of the world to human rights abuses. Musician and human rights advocate Peter Gabriel co-founded Witness in 1992.

Professional photographer Chase Jarvis offers 12 tips for making better images using a variety of gear from point-and- shoot cameras using natural light, to shooting with a high-qual- ity digital SLR camera. Worth a look because of the tips such as attaching a camera to a skateboard: www.youtube.com/watch?v=-6zK6cz52CI&NR=1.

Taking stills with the iPhone. A helpful BBC video about taking stills: www.youtube.com/watch?v=uJlMuGXQ-Dg.

CHAPTER 6: RECORDING LOCATION SOUND USING A SMARTPHONE

A helpful BBC video about recording good audio with an iPhone (almost four minutes): www.youtube.com/watch?v=q8ngvpZwxDg.

Here is a useful companion story about recording audio, by Lindsay Kalter: http://ijnet.org/blog/how-record-clear-audio-mobile-phone.

Videos about Presentation Skills

The BBC has posted a series of six videos on YouTube to teach reporters about presentation skills. Go to the first and then watch the other five in the order the BBC recommends: www.youtube.com/watch?v=JHT2R4e4-Po&list=PLBD733239ED78941C&index.

CHAPTER 7: SCRAP: THE ELEMENTS OF MOJO STORYTELLING

Neal Augenstein is a reporter with PBS in the United States. He maintains a website devoted to mobile reporting: http://iphone-reporting.com/.

Quinn's iBook published in April 2014 might be useful as a guide to writing scripts: *CLARITY: A Guide to Clear Writing*. Available at: https://itunes.apple.com/gb/book/clarity/id843307803.

CHAPTER 8: MOJO INTERVIEWING

This BBC training video has tips on asking questions relative to the kind of person being interviewed (runs for ten minutes): www.youtube.com/watch?v=EWmDHH9sWeU.

In this video, producer Drew Keller talks about the importance of good research as preparation for an interview (runs six minutes): www.youtube.com/watch?v=4gmV-OlmEsc.

Katie Couric gives her tips on how to conduct a good interview (runs five minutes): www.youtube.com/watch?v=4eOynrl2eTM.

D.J. Clark of CCTV offers advice on video interviewing in this program (runs 9.19 minutes): www.youtube.com/watch?v=i7JlBr92wKg.

CHAPTER 9: EDITING ON A SMARTPHONE

The BBC offers a "one-minute" guide to a range of skills, including the magic of editing: www.bbc.co.uk/films/oneminutemovies/howto/edit.shtml.

David Burns, a media professor at Salisbury University in the United States, presents this useful video on editing for visual effect: http://ijnet.org/video/how-edit-visual-sequences-effective-video-storytelling.

CHAPTER 10: POST-PRODUCTION ON A SMARTPHONE

Ivo offers an excellent video on editing and iMovie (runs 8:41): www.youtube.com/watch?v=z13NXAmlccA.

CHAPTER 11: MOJO, SOCIAL NETWORKS AND SOCIAL MEDIA

The executive summary of the 2014 *Global Digital Media Trendbook* is free at http://wnmn.org/wp-content/uploads/2014/08/WNMN_ExecutiveSummary_14.pdf.

Vadim Lavrusik, Facebook's journalism program manager, wrote the guide "Best Practices for Journalists on Facebook": www.facebook.com/notes/facebook-journalists/best-practices-for-journalists-on-facebook/593586440653374.

Lavrusik also penned "Improving Conversations on Facebook with Replies" aimed at users, at www.facebook.com/notes/journalists-on-facebook/improving-conversations-on-facebook-with-replies/578890718789613.

Details of the media release "Facebook partners with Storify to provide a news agency" at http://newsroom.fb.com/news/2014/04/announcing-fb-newswire-powered-by-storyful/.

Twitter media blog: https://blog.twitter.com/media.

Twitter service for journalists: https://media.twitter.com/.

CHAPTER 12: FILE DELIVERY AND PHONE MANAGEMENT

Learn all about the difference between bits, bytes, nibbles and gigabits at these Wikipedia sites: http://en.wikipedia.org/wiki/Megabyte and http://en.wikipedia.org/wiki/Data_rate_units.

Google has published a series of country reports about consumer behavior and smartphones. Full data sets and country reports based on research conducted in 2013 at http://think.withgoogle.com/mobileplanet/en/downloads/.

CHAPTER 13: ETHICS AND LEGAL ASPECTS OF MOJO

Ethics Guidelines

The WGBH Educational Foundation produces the excellent TV and online documentary series Frontline. WGBH is a major producer of programs for PBS, the US public television network. Read Frontline's journalism guidelines here: www.pbs.org/wgbh/pages/frontline/about-us/journalistic-guidelines/.

Early in 2014 the Online News Association started a project called "Do it yourself ethics code" designed to allow journalists to create or customize codes that reflect their views of journalism. Read about the project at http://journalists.org/2014/07/16/first-round-of-crowdsourcing-adds-depth-to-diy-ethics-code-project/.

Legal Resources

The BBC Academy offers an excellent resource on contempt of court. Though focused on the UK, the principles are useful. www.bbc.co.uk/academy/journalism/article/art20130702112133630

In August 2014 David Banks published a 19-page booklet "The legal risks of UGC: A hands-on guide to copyright, defamation and other legal issues for publishers of user-generated content." The publisher is cOntent (correct spelling) and you can find it at www.facebook.com/n0ticenearby/posts/811857098838019.

The BBC published a round-up of legal issues at www.bbc.co.uk/blogs/blogcollegeofjournalism/posts/Managing-the-legal-risks-of-UGC-Key-issues-to-consider.

Ivo Burum's iBook *How to Mojo* includes a section on staying legally healthy with easy to follow tips.

The Canadian national broadcaster CBC has published guidelines on secret recording: www.cbc.radio-canada.ca/en/reporting-to-canadians/acts-and-policies/programming/journalism/clandestine/.

Articles by Mojo Reporters (Includes Tips)

Neal Augenstein of America's PBS is a mojo specialist. Read his piece about shooting video: http://wtop.com/256/3430371/Pro-tips-How-to-shoot-video-with-your-phone.

Also helpful is Charlotte Latimer's quite long article entitled "How to Produce Video on Your Mobile Phone": www.journalism.co.uk/skills/how-to-produce-videos-on-your-mobile-phone/s7/a553911/.

Lauren Hockenson penned a useful piece entitled "How to Shoot Video from a Smartphone Like a Pro" at www.mediabistro.com/10000words/how-to-shoot-video-from-a-smartphone-like-a-pro_b16497.

UK Sky TV reporter Nic Martin offers advice about mobile phone reporting in this article: www.newsrewired.com/2012/02/03/newsrw-three-pieces-of-advice-for-mobile-reporting-from-skys-nick-martin/.

Sites and Books about Multi-Media Journalism

Mark Briggs has written a free book about multi-media, available as a pdf. The book, *Journalism 2.0: How to Survive and Thrive (A Digital Literacy Guide for the Information Age)* is a little dated but Chapters 9 and 10 are still relevant for learning about video: http://www.kcnn.org/resources/journalism_20/.

Mindy McAdams, professor of journalism technologies at the University of Florida, has a personal blog about teaching online journalism. Some of the links in the left-hand column of her site are useful for mojos: http://mindymcadams.com/tojou/.

Some years ago Mark S. Luckie created an excellent blog about multi-media, 10000words.net. It has evolved onto the Media Bistro site and is a useful read for developments in US media: www.mediabistro.com/10000words/.

British journalism academic Paul Bradshaw maintains an excellent blog, which often contains posts about mobile journalism: http://onlinejournalismblog.com/.

Videos about Backpack Journalism

Independent journalist Bill Gentile offers two useful videos about backpack journalism. Note that this is different from mojo or mobile journalism, but some of the tips in the videos are helpful for mojos.

Part 1: http://ijnet.org/video/part-1-bill-gentile-backpack-journalism.

Part 2: http://ijnet.org/video/part-2-bill-gentile-essentials-backpack-journalists.

Feature Films Made with the iPhone

One of the first feature films made only with an iPhone was Paranmanjang in South Korea (translates as Night Fishing). Brothers Park Chan-wook and Park Chan-kyong directed, produced and wrote this feature, which runs for 33 minutes. Paranmanjang was shot entirely on several iPhone 4s in 2011, and was funded by KT, at the time South Korea's exclusive iPhone distributor. This movie won the Golden Bear for Best Short at the 61st Berlin international film festival in 2011. See www.youtube.com/watch?v=2tRlqPQ7dAw.

The Fixer (2012) has won many awards at film competitions. Its budget was $US400. Watch (it runs 7.15) at www.thesmalls.com/film/fixer.

The Mumbai Mantra runs 2.56 and is quirky and interesting. You can watch it at http://vimeo.com/93138715.

Kalapukan, translated as Mud Place, is an intriguing 2.56 video shot entirely with an iPhone 4 in southern Philippines in 2012: http://vimeo.com/33658367.

AUTHOR BIOGRAPHIES

Ivo Burum is an award-winning television writer, director, executive producer and journalist with more than 30 years' experience across a range of program styles. He has produced television stories in more than 35 countries including for frontline current affairs series such as *Foreign Correspondent*. A video journalist and a pioneer of the user-generated style of production, Ivo has spent three decades empowering people to produce their own self-shot video stories.

His mobile journalism workshops in remote communities, for education and with mainstream media, were developed form the lessons learned on self-shot television series. He has trained professional journalists from Norway, Denmark, UK, Timor and Australia, to mojo. From 2012 to 2013, Ivo was the mobile training lead at *Ekstra Bladet* in Denmark. Dr Burum lectures in multimedia journalism at Deakin University in Australia. His PhD research was focused on mobile storytelling across spheres of communication and he's regularly invited to speak on mobile and convergent journalism. His publications include book chapters, academic papers and an iBook on mobile journalism. This is his second book. Dr Burum runs Burum Media, a mobile journalism and web TV consultancy and writes regularly on mobile journalism in industry magazines. He writes two blogs focused on convergent media and his websites are www.smartmojo.com and www.burummedia.com.au, and his Twitter is @citizenmojo. Examples of his mojo work can be found at www.youtube.com/user/howtomojo.

Stephen Quinn is professor of journalism at the Norwegian College of Creative Studies in Oslo. In the past six years he has taught journalism students and media professionals how to make broadcast-quality videos using only an iPhone in 16 countries. Dr Quinn runs MOJO Media Insights, a digitally focused company based in Brighton in the United Kingdom. Examples of his videos can be found at http://www.youtube.com/ningbomojo. Dr Quinn was the digital development editor at the *South China Morning Post* from 2011 until 2013. At the *Post* he helped re-launch the site that in November 2012 won the WAN/Ifra gold medal for best news website. From 1996 to 2011 Dr Quinn, who has an Australian passport, was a journalism professor at universities in Australia, the United Arab Emirates, the United States and China. Between 1975 and 1995 Dr Quinn was a journalist with six daily newspapers including the *Bangkok Post* and *The Guardian* in the UK, the Australian Broadcasting Corporation, the UK's Press Association, BBC-TV, ITN and TVNZ. This is his twenty-first print book. He has published four digital books using Apple's iBooks Author software, and also shows people how to make iBooks. Dr Quinn co-writes a weekly wine column syndicated to seven daily newspapers and a range of magazines in Asia and Europe.

INDEX